On Intricacy

On Intricacy

The Work of John Meunier Architect

Edited by Patrick Lynch

Canalside Press

For Dotty

"The being of art cannot be defined as an object of aesthetic consciousness, because, on the contrary, the aesthetic attitude is more than it knows of itself. It is part of the event of being that occurs in presentation, and belongs essentially to play as play... What we mean by truth here can best be defined again in terms of our concept of play. The weight of the things we encounter in understanding plays itself out in a linguistic event, a play of words playing around and about what is learnt. Language games exist where we as learners—and when do we cease to be that?— rise to the understanding of the world. Here it is worth recalling what we said about the nature of play, namely that the player's actions should not be considered subjective actions, since it is, rather, the game itself that plays, for it draws the players into itself and thus becomes the actual subjectum of the playing.... When we understand a text, what is meaningful in it captivates us just as the beautiful captivates us... what we encounter in the experience of the beautiful and in understanding the meaning of tradition really has something of the truth of play about it."

—Hans-Georg Gadamer, *Truth and Method*[1]

THE LONG GAME

On Intricacy is perhaps unusual in that it's not a monograph, nor is it a hagiography. John Meunier is still alive. *On Intricacy* celebrates and proselytises the ideas that Meunier has articulated throughout his career. *On Intricacy* is not a book about him as such, nor simply a book by him, but a book with him, and it reflects his life's work as an architect and teacher, in the UK and USA.

On Intricacy is concerned with the deep reciprocity of ethics and aesthetics in human ecology and culture. Intricacy is not so much an aesthetic term—although it is a sign of quality in artistic work—as something intrinsic to human situations. Intricacy is something that architecture does or doesn't reflect, and when it does, it tends to be life-like, vital, and therefore good.

On Intricacy is a visual and written polemic reflecting the hard-won wisdom of a practical life. *On Intricacy* is also a biography of sorts of a man born into a relatively recent, but also a very different age. It tells an inspiring story from a period of hope and opportunity in the 20th century. *On Intricacy* is an anthology. An anthology is a collection of flowers[2], often offered at a festival. *On Intricacy* is an invitation to share in the deeper meaning of theory[3]: to participate in a form of long game that demands that we give ourselves up to it, witness it, and join in with it; keeping alive the possibility of architecture that "really has something of the truth of play about it".[4]

—Patrick Lynch

Contents

An Intricate Building

John Meunier

Has a rich array of scales, from that of the hand, the foot, the arm, and the body, up to the scale of the city or landscape of which it is a part.

Rewards the senses: sight, sound, touch, smell, through its orchestration of light and shade, silence and echo, rough and smooth, cool and warm, high and low, close and far, soft and hard, simple and complex scents.

Both conceals and exposes. Is both diverse and unified.

Like an Intricate city, can have multiple authors, so it can include older structures, but it must be coherent.

May derive its Intricacy from the interaction between its formal language and a rich program, its physical and social context, and its technology.

Not only responds to but also contributes to the richness of the culture of which it is a part. It accepts and celebrates its role in a historical continuum.

Can be compared to serious music, literature, film, art in that it rewards multiple encounters.

Is rich in resonances with other phenomena and experience.

May be formally complex or formally simple, but it cannot be incoherent or banal.

The Intricate Work of Architecture

Patrick Lynch

"...the theory of
 Poetry is the theory of life."
—Wallace Stevens, *An Ordinary Evening in New Haven*

"Work is restrained desire."
—Hans-Georg Gadamer[1]

We have some funny ideas about the relationship between theory and practise today, especially in architecture, tending to typify the former as writing, and the latter as building. However, one very obvious distinction of architecture—in contrast to construction in general, which is mostly carried out by non-architects —is that architecture is Intricate work: we don't make it as such, but we think it, we draw it, we imagine it into being. We propose and we predict, with the pretty audacious idea, that expectations which we imagine will be met. Architecture involves courage and premonition, building with theory, building with risk. In the life and career of John Meunier the theory and practise of architecture are strands of one long intertwined thread, a rope even. These strands are impossible to separate, and as a consequence are incredibly strong, capable of supporting great swings of fate, and an unusual amount of cultural weight.

A number of recently famous and significant architects' work has seemingly grown fully formed out of theory. Yet a lot of this work renounces the practical character of architecture entirely, seeing the art of architecture, in line with the Kantian definition of art per se, as typified by its distinct a lack of usefulness. This top-down approach, whereby theory is applied to the world via design operations on it, might be said to express a formalistic and systematic misunderstanding not only of the practical character of art and design, but also of the situated and dialogical nature of theory. The German philosopher Hans-Georg Gadamer describes the difference between a modern understanding of theory i.e. instrumental knowledge designed to predict and to ensure results, and the original meaning of theoria in the ancient world i.e. participation in the order of the cosmos. In this ancient understanding, theory is not distinct from practise.

The character of praxis is closely related to both practical everyday life, Gadmer claims, and furthermore to festive time. A participant in an ancient Greek festival was called a "theoros", Gadamer reminds us, and so he is able to define theory as "true participation; not something active but something passive (pathos), namely being totally involved in and carried away by what one sees". Modern theory does not define itself in terms of passive participation, but rather as an aggressive form of productive knowledge. In the discipline of architectural education and culture, the goal of theory is most often the desire to assert the dominance of reason; it is ordinarily manifest in systematic architecture, typified by an architecture that attempts to assert its autonomy from human situations and ecology. Theory has become simultaneously divorced from practical life and somehow imbued with a spirit of automatic production— it is as if theory can stand in for experience and craft in assuring the success of an act of imagination. The character of this production is curiously sealed off from the traditional relationship between skill and luck that typifies the classical concept of creativity, and also from the traditional character of artistic work as a kind of "self knowledge" .

Gadamer explicates Hegel's notion of "Practical Bildung" (or Practical Education/Cultivation) in his *Phenomenology of Spirit*, relating this both to training and to the cultivation of selfhood:

"Work is restrained desire. In forming the object—that is, in being selflessly active and concerned with a universal—working consciousness raises itself above the immediacy of its existence to universality; or, as Hegel puts it, by forming the thing it forms itself. What he means is that in acquiring a 'capacity', a skill, man gains a sense of himself... It (Practical Bildung) is found in the circumspection that, while concerned with the individual situation or business, remains open to observing what else might be necessary... For every profession has something about it of fate, of external necessity; it demands that one gives oneself to tasks that one would not seek out as a private aim. Practical Bildung is seen in one's fulfilling one's profession wholly, in all its aspects. But this includes overcoming the element in it that is alien to the particular which is oneself, and making it wholly one's own. Thus to give oneself to the universality of a profession is at the same time 'to know how to limit oneself—i.e., to make one's profession one's concern. Then it is no longer a limitation'... Theoretical Bildung leads beyond what man knows and experiences immediately. It consists in learning to recognise what is different from oneself... Bildung always involves the development of theoretical interests... To recognise one's own in the alien, to become home in it, is the basic movement of spirit, whose being consists in returning to itself from what is other."

Gadamer suggests then, extending Hegel's argument, that as "restrained desire" professional work is a form of self-discipline and of discovery; travel away from one's origins and towards a form of mature selfhood. Practical Education might be said, therefore, to be at once an intensely physical and ontological form of movement. In this understanding of theoretical practice, skill and self-awareness are united with "learning to recognise what is different

from oneself...". Understood as knowledge of the other, Gadamer (and Hegel) suggest that the practical character of education and theory implicitly points to the ethical dimension of the imagination.

In contrast, the misapplication of a modern understanding of theory to architecture usually represents today an abnegation of the ethical, economic and ecological character of praxis. It is the result, I think, of a misunderstanding of the practical character of theoretical architectural knowledge. Architecture is a utile art, and so cannot, does not, and should not fit into the neat categorical silos of Theory vs. Practise.

The work of John Meunier is evidence that architectural theory can grow out of, and is deepened and enriched by, the practical experience of architectural design, and vice versa. This may seem obvious to any architect, yet it is impossible today for a young teacher to gain tenure as both a theoretician and as a professor of practice; the one precludes the other today. The story of a life lived as a teacher and as an architect (that this book recounts) is almost inconceivable today; yet the practical wisdom that John Meunier communicates is precious and vital. The ideas presented in this book might be said to be a form of practical theory. Our hope is that students, teachers and architects might engage with it in an attempt to appreciate the heuristic and situated nature of architectural knowledge, and in particular its Intricate character. What the authors of this book suggest, and which John Meunier's work as a teacher and architect posits, is an idea that architecture might be described simultaneously as practical and theoretical, and thus Intricate; what follows is an exposition, explanation and example of the Intricate character of architectural work.

Opposite, top to bottom:
Meunier at his Caldecote home
Students working at Meunier's house in Cincinnati

The Intricate Work of Architecture   17

Intricacy and Collaboration in my Work with Others

John Meunier

Collaboration is not limited to work with fellow design professionals but is an aspect of the Intricacy of human relationships generally. Architectural Intricacy can, and often does, emerge from such Intricate creative relationships.

I do, however, make a distinction between working with other designers as collaborative partners in the synthesis towards a coherent, hopefully Intricate, design, and, on the other hand, working in collaboration with clients[1], consultants, regulators, contractors and sub-contractors, all of whom will introduce potentially valuable information and concepts, including constraints, which can be stimulants, and the raw material, towards the richness and complexity of an Intricate design. One of my definitions of Intricacy being Coherent Complexity.

The majority of my professional design work was undertaken in partnership with other architects, a process that I found, on the whole, to be very productive. Architectural ideas emerge and develop until they almost have a life of their own; they then need to be served by an expanding team as they move towards implementation in built form.

However, the Meunier House belongs to that special case where the lone architect and the client are the same person—almost. A proviso being that

there are obviously others involved, notably, for their home, the architect's life-partner or spouse. In this case my wife, as a client, has her fingerprints all over the building, partly because of her insistence on functionality, particularly, for example, the necessity for convenient storage. The net result is a small house with a large amount of built-in storage, with a distinction made between immediately accessible short-term storage and less accessible longer-term storage. That may be because, as an American, my wife was used to basements and attics as well as built-in 'closets'. This house has neither a basement (cellar), nor an attic, but it has a lot of built-in closets (cupboards), with the longer-term storage being at higher level over the immediately accessible storage below, behind standard height doors. The closets are not in the rooms but are a part of the thick partitions between rooms. The storage of the eating and drinking equipment is in a pair of cabinets between the kitchen and the dining area, accessible on both sides, and the full height wood box that holds up one side of those cabinets contains not only drainage and vent pipes, but also cleaning supplies and brushes; the wood of the storage complementing the colour and texture of the raw fletton brick walls [2].

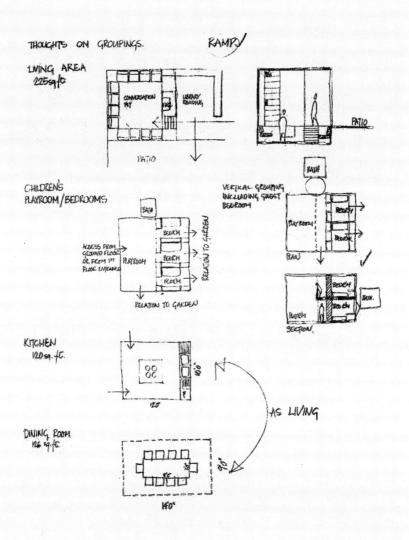

THOUGHTS ON GROUPINGS.

RAMP

LIVING AREA
225 sq. ft.

CONVERSATION PIT

LIBRARY READING

PATIO

PATIO

CHILDREN'S
PLAYROOM / BEDROOMS

BATH

ACCESS FROM
GROUND FLOOR
OR FROM 1ST
FLOOR ENTRANCE

PLAYROOM

BEDRM

BEDRM

BEDRM

RELATION TO GARDEN

RELATION TO GARDEN

VERTICAL GROUPING
INCLUDING GUEST
BEDROOM

BATH

PLAYROOM

BEDRM

BEDRM

PLAN

BEDRM

PLAYRM

BATH.

BEDRM

SECTION.

KITCHEN
120 sq. ft.

10'0"

120

DINING ROOM
126 sq. ft.

AS LIVING

9'0"

14'0"

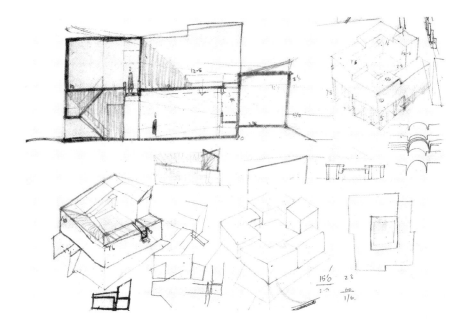

The design of the Wendon house, that initiated my partnership with my then new colleague at Cambridge University School of Architecture, Barry Gasson, was conducted via a series of conversations with the clients, meetings for which we prepared a number of discussion boards. On this first board, we added at the meeting two comments: "RAMP" and "AS LIVING". These comments were key to the generation of what Viollet le Duc calls the "Chief Ruling Idea" of the house. The comments emerged during the discussion with the clients as we talked with them about possible changes of level to articulate the different activity spaces, starting with a discussion of a living room having two different functions: a communal gathering and a private reading area, with a different vertical scale for each. The second sketch, drawn after that meeting, explores the use of changing levels and ramps spiralling up within the house.

For the Wendon House we had two clients, husband and wife, but what became clear was that the husband, John Wendon, had another motive than

patio   wc
kitchen
study
barton   children
garden
family   entry
baths   parents
living   new road
cambridge   guests
dining
laundry

gardenfamilystudyguestscnildrenbathwcentrylaundryparentsbathkitchendininglivingpatio

garden family study guests children bath wc entry laundry parents bath kitchen dining living pati

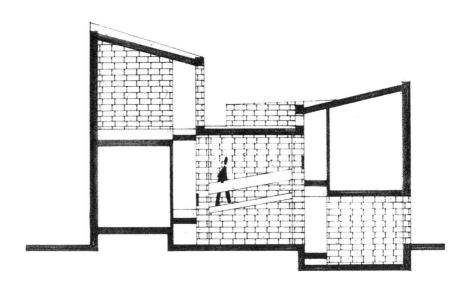

building a home for his family. He had obtained the franchise for a ceiling heating system and this house was to be both a demonstration and an advertisement for the use of that system. So, for him, the publication of the house in many different magazines, both nationally and internationally, and its selection by the British Council for exhibition at the 1967 Paris Biennale was the fulfillment of an ambition beyond his brief to create a home. The fact that they sold the house after only a couple of years of occupancy, and built a more traditional house next door, suggests that the other client, his wife, was not so satisfied.

But the story has a happy ending, as the house was eventually bought by another architect, the then Chief Architect of the Cambridgeshire County Council, Viren Sahai, who made some sensitive additions and modifications, and lived and painted there until he died. The architect's German born widow, Ingrid, still enjoys the house, and even though I must admit to some misgivings on revisiting a work so obviously modified by others, I am reconciled to this as an example of the sort of complexity that the world almost inevitably imposes on the work of an architect, a complexity that, in the right hands, can enhance its Intricacy.

John Meunier

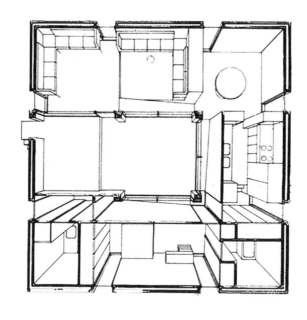

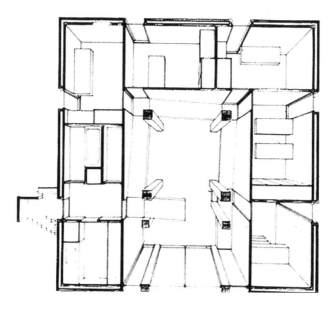

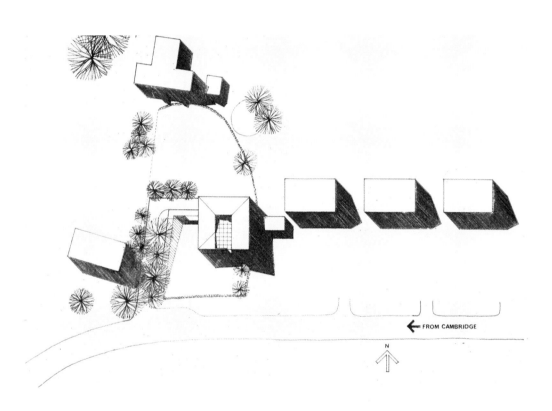

FROM CAMBRIDGE

N

The Burrell Museum was not only at a totally different scale and programme from these houses, it also began as a two-stage competition, and so there was at first no direct contact with the primary client, the City of Glasgow and its representatives. There was a very thoughtful and well prepared programme, prepared, we later discovered, by three nationally distinguished architects— Bill Howell, Philip Dowson, and Theo Crosby—on behalf of the city. We never got to meet these architects in that role; who we did eventually get to meet were members of the curatorial staff of the museum, the chief curator and the curators of the various areas of the collection. One of my most vivid memories was being handed some beautiful piece, from its storage in a car barn in the city, by the relevant curator and having it explained to us as we held it. That was the most perfect museum experience and it has always lived with me as we have designed encounters with objects. The closer we can get to that direct experience, the better. In other words, the less we can put between the observer and the object, and also the more we were able to see the object in daylight and in a natural setting, the better. But daylight is, of course, problematic as it contains wavelengths such

This page: Exhibits at the Burrell
Opposite: Additions made to the Wendon House

Intricacy and Collaboration in my Work with Others 35

as ultra-violet and infra-red that are destructive to organic materials. Stained glass is not organic and can be seen directly in sun-light, so we placed it on the south face of the museum. The tapestries, one of the marvels of Sir William Burrell's collection, are however very susceptible to light damage, so they are placed in the centre, well away from natural light, while the more robust pieces are displayed against the cool filtered light on the north face against the background of a shaded woodland. For us it was the curators, and the objects themselves, who were our most important clients, along with the visitors exploring the museum and seeking rich engagements with the objects in its collection. All of them adding to the complexity and challenging our ability to achieve coherence, and thus Intricacy. It may be because I have lived most of my professional life as a design teacher and have found myself focused on helping my students identify the seeds of an architectural idea in their own thinking, and working with them to develop that idea into a feasible architectural proposition, that I am comfortable with the idea of multiple authorship as long as the ultimate goal is coherent complexity, or Intricacy, in the work.

There seems to be a problem, partly psychological perhaps, partly cultural, in positing the idea of creativity as often fundamentally collaborative. There is a more or less natural human tendency to claim ownership of ideas as we seek credit and admiration from others. But that can be counterproductive. As a teacher I have often found myself attempting to stop my students from explaining their work by saying, "I wanted to do this or that"; requiring of them other more substantial justifications for the validity of their work. If an idea is good and has potential towards contributing to the success of the task at hand, then its ownership is not important, and it can be developed by colleagues with enthusiasm and creativity.

Developed towards what though? That is the key question. The answer may simply be "a good work of architecture", but then we inevitably ask ourselves, "what constitutes a good work of architecture?" I have spent the last few years of my life attempting to address this question as I have pursued the notion of Intricacy in architecture and the built environment.

It is probably appropriate for me to write a few words about my role in the design of The Burrell Museum, for which my former business and design partner, Barry Gasson, has appropriately received the most credit[3]; Barry was the initiator of the work and the leading architect through to the end of the project.

The Burrell Museum was the subject of a design competition in two phases. The first phase was an open competition, in which many architects, including some very eminent names, competed. Out of that phase six projects were chosen for the second limited phase. The winner of that phase was not automatically awarded the commission. Barry had decided to enter the competition on his own and after visiting the site made the very important decision to position the building against the tree line on the diagonal north side of the large meadow. As the deadline drew near, he realized he needed some help in preparing the complete submission and invited me to participate. He and I had been partners on many projects, both built and unbuilt over the preceding years, including the Wendon House, the Essex Sports Pavilion, the Edington House, the Heacham Housing project, a development plan and some student housing for Trinity Hall,

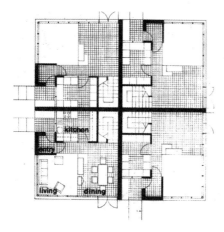 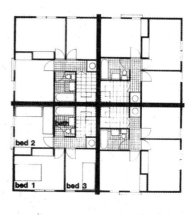

and the redesign of the entry sequence for the Cambridge Arts Theatre. We won that first phase and were invited, as a partnership, Gasson and Meunier Architects, to enter the second phase, which we also won. Then it was a question whether we should be awarded the commission, no sure thing, as we were still in our thirties and had no large buildings in our portfolio. Happily, we received the support of the architectural advisors to the competition, because of our track record together, and as a partnership we were awarded the commission. Despite some growing animosity I remained in the partnership and worked on the design until the end of Design Development, at which point it was clear that the partnership should not continue, and the project was completed under Barry Gasson's leadership.

The breakdown of any relationship is painful, but sometimes the individuals who have happily and productively worked together for several years do grow apart. Their lives, relationships, and developing responsibilities take different paths. I remain grateful for the productive and Intricate creative partnership that I had with Barry Gasson, and others, and this volume and the thoughts within it, are partly about that work.

It was at about that stage that I was appointed by New Hall, Cambridge—now Murray Edwards College—as the architect for a revised overall plan for the College, including revisions to one of the existing courts and some new Student Housing, on which I invited another colleague, David Handlin, to act as a collaborator.

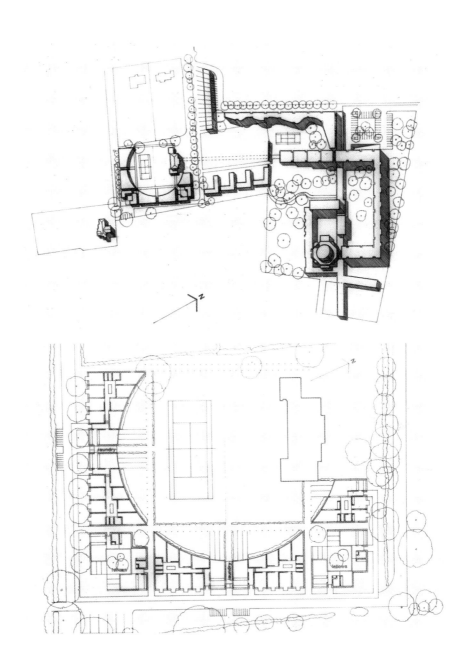

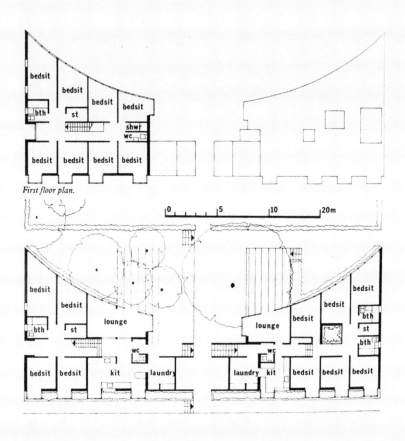

bedsit

bedsit

bedsit

bedsit

bth

st

shwr

wc

bedsit | bedsit | bedsit | bedsit

First floor plan.

0   5   10   20m

bedsit

bedsit

bth

st

lounge

wc

bedsit | bedsit | kit | laundry

lounge

bedsit

bedsit

bth

st

bth

wc

laundry | kit | bedsit | bedsit | bedsit

On Intricacy:
An Amicable Prolegomena

John Meunier and Patrick Lynch

"Intricacy is that part which serves to correct the excess of simplicity
falling into meanness."
—William Hogarth[1]

"It is not sufficient that the principle masses of the composition are
well considered. The attention, study and labour of the architect must
extend to the smallest, subaltern and accessory parts of his work."
—Sir John Soane[2]

JM: For many years, as a teacher of architecture, I have suggested to my
students that the distinction that one might draw between run-of-the mill
buildings, and those that deserve to be called architecture, is that the latter
reward contemplation; that the more one observes them, interacts with them,
looks carefully at them and thinks about them, the more benefit one draws
from them both emotionally and intellectually.

I do not accept the distinction that the art historian Nikolaus Pevsner
once drew[1], in attempting to make a similar distinction, between a cathedral
and a bicycle shed. It seems to me that the first could be banal, and the

second exquisitely conceived. The latter resonating with the technological sophistication of its occupants, the freedoms that the machines brought not only to men, but to women and children; thoughtfully scaled and responsive to its setting, recognising, as a really good car-park might, that people arrive as riders and leave as pedestrians; while at the same time, inventively addressing the basic needs for shelter and security. If the bicycle shed operated on all these fronts, then I would claim that it deserved recognition as architecture.

More recently, visits to desert cities around the world (in search of lessons that could improve the quality and performance of our newer desert cities, such as Greater Phoenix, in Arizona, where I have lived and worked for a quarter of a century), have alerted me to those qualities that make a city rewarding, particularly to the pedestrian exploring both the public and the private realms. In some ways these qualities are similar to the ones I have attempted to indicate above; that cities should enrich the experience and understanding of those who live in and explore them, through their layering of scales, engagement of the emotions, their climate, their history and their culture.

The term that seems to me to capture the quality that both a good piece of architecture, and a good city must have, is Intricacy.

The word, and the idea, are of course not unique. Others have pursued them. In particular I was interested to learn of an exhibit at the Institute of Contemporary Art at the University of Pennsylvania in 2003 organised by Greg Lynn whose title was *Intricacy*. The exhibit focused primarily on recent developments in art, and to a certain extent in architecture, influenced largely by recent digital and genetic engineering developments. This work is not irrelevant to my interests, but it is not central. I am in agreement with the following:

> "Among artists, designers, and architects there is an emerging sensibility of intricacy. Partially heralded by the digital and genetic engineering revolutions, the term intricacy connotes a new model of connectionism composed of extremely small scale and incredibly diverse elements. Intricacy is the fusion of disparate elements into

continuity, the becoming whole of components that retain their status as pieces of a larger composition. Unlike simple hierarchy, subdivision, compartmentalisation or modularity, intricacy involves a variation of the parts that is not reducible to the structure of the whole."[2]

Intricacy is not to be confused with complexity. I am, of course, familiar with Robert Venturi's *Complexity and Contradiction in Architecture*.[3] But unlike Venturi, who was "rebelling against the purism of modernism", and whose work heralded a major stylistic shift towards the neo-traditionalism that still dominates the so-called New Urbanism (a shift that arguably owes more to the Krier brothers than it does to Venturi), my goal is not to promote any particular mode of or style of design, it is to argue in favour of density, and for coherence.

Complexity and Intricacy are of course related, but I would argue that there is a distinction, that Intricacy is a special sub-set of Complexity where Coherence has been achieved.

Here is my current definition: Intricacy is an intellectual construct that interprets a challenging set of perceived phenomena within a rich structure of relationships that link each member of the set consequentially to the rest.

An object is perceived as Intricate when its comprehension requires intellectual engagement. Such an object may have complex form, but it can also be Intricate because of its ambiguity or significance. Multiple readings of simple forms may also imply Intricacy. Intricacy is a general aspect of aesthetic experience, and not necessarily a formal characteristic. In my view, works of art in every genre (visual arts, music, literature, architecture, etc.) must necessarily be "Intricate" in order to have long-term, lasting cultural significance. Their formal structure and their multiple layers of meaning may separately, or together, achieve the quality of Intricacy. It is this quality that lends major works the ability to reward those who revisit them many times.

An object of our attention is perceived as Intricate when its comprehension requires and rewards such intellectual engagement.

PL: A deeper dimension of creative culture is implied by the notion of Intricacy I think. It points towards ancient philosophical concepts that underlie ontology and mathematics: Diversity and Unity, the One and the Many, Identity and Difference. Architecture encompasses both speculative and symbolic geometry of course, and in Alberti's formulation architecture is a form of moral philosophy[4] (rather than a science or an art directly). Intricacy is found both in poetry and mathematics, and when we come across it in good architecture, we are reminded of its origins in both.

In fact, Intricacy is as much a temporal dimension as a physical characteristic of an art work, and fundamentally it reveals the primacy of the experiential character of art experience. One might call this an aspect of spatiality, since time is involved in this, of course, and cognition and memory, the past and the future, as well as the horizon of the present.[5] Intricacy is a phenomenon.

JM: As architects, if we are artists, our job is to create buildings that not only meet an array of pragmatic needs, but also intrigue, challenge, and ultimately reward, emotionally, sensually, and intellectually, those who experience our work. What follows is an effort to pursue this definition as it might relate to different aspects of architecture and urbanism. We will be considering both elements that can contribute to the generation of Intricacy, such as Program, Technology, Form (my interpretation of the Vitruvian triad of Commoditas, Firmitas, and Venustas), History, Religion, Iconography, Simile and Metaphor, as well as the ways in which Intricacy can be achieved through Sequence, Layering, Contrast, Scale, Proportion, Tactility, Ornament and Decoration.

We find endless examples of Intricacy in the natural world, and nature has been used not only as a model by architects such as Frank Lloyd Wright, but also as a partner in the design of Intricate environments (whether as the complementary park or garden, as the plants that intertwine with the pergolas and trellises on the outer edges of our buildings, or as the integrated component of green walls or roofs that are currently being incorporated in an effort to achieve a more sustainable environment).

JM: All buildings contain stories. Good architecture tells stories. There are the human stories about who built them and why, what challenges had to be overcome in the building of them, how they were occupied and used, how did they respond to changes in both use and context. And then there are the technical stories about how they were built and what with …. and so on.

What we are discussing here, however, are the carefully contrived, Intricate, architectural stories that a building can tell in the hands of a good designer; we are talking about the architectural analogue or equivalent of a play, a piece of classical music, or a well contrived work of literature.

An architectural story uses the elements of a building—columns, beams, arches, rough and smooth stones, flat and curved walls, doors and windows, and the light and spaces between them—as the equivalent of the protagonists, instruments, intervals and sounds, characters, and their relationships in works of drama, music, and literature. Giulio Romano's Palazzo del Te and The Scottish Parliament Building by Enric Miralles are two examples of buildings that tell architectural stories, and which achieve a form of spatial and intellectual Intricacy.

In the courtyard of the Palazzo del Te, on two of the four walls, there are triglyphs that look as though they are dropping out of the entablature in a very wilful way.

So, what is the story in the Palazzo del Te that holds this all together in an Intricate way? One might suggest that there is a literary plot that tells a story of a journey from the world (the exterior) to paradise (the garden) via purgatory (the transitional courtyard), and that the drama of the dropped triglyph and the battle between the wall and the column symbolizes the struggle and pain of that purifying transition.

Whether that Christian literary plot was intended, and the extraordinary frescoes on the interior of the Palazzo suggest another based on classical mythology, it is more important here to claim a purely architectural story that

takes us from a heavy, wall dominated, exterior, where the weight of the wall is emphasized through rustication, through an intermediary courtyard where the heavy rough wall is being replaced by a partly smoother wall and with half-round columns supporting a stressed entablature, emphasised on the main axis by the dropped triglyphs, to a garden façade that is both wholly smooth, with freestanding columns supporting arches, as well as a summary of much of the story as it proceeds from the ends to the centre. The two courtyard porticos are further transitions between each of these polarities. The one heavy, dark and rough, the other light, bright, and smooth. Although there are many very different architectural gestures, this 'plot', that is about sequence and transformation, pulls them all together as a whole. There is both Complexity and Coherence. There are convincing arguments therefore for the presence of Intricacy.

There is no question that The Scottish Parliament Building is complex, but is it Intricate? The complexity is immediately apparent. There is nothing simple here. More than fifty percent of its area is in landscape rather than building. It incorporates an old building, Queensbury House. It has a rich palette of materials: wood, concrete, stones both light and dark, painted steel, gleaming metal sheet roofing, clear glass or glass with a thin layer of wood veneer. It has a wide array of forms: straight and curved, vertical and angled, repeated and varied, shallow and deep, smooth and textured, rounded and sharply pointed. The façades are multi-layered. Joints and window mullions and muntins are often discontinuous. Potentially large elements are nearly always elaborated so that their scale is reduced. Natural light is introduced both directly and indirectly. Artificial lights are clustered and dispersed, hung at many different levels or emerging out of recesses, holes and slots. Similar spaces are never exactly the same. The circulation is oblique and indirect. The largest space, the Debating Chamber, is hard to identify from outside and not easy to find inside.

So, what are the characteristics that would qualify it as Intricate architecture? Does it have an architectural story to tell? Is it coherent in the sense that there are convincing relationships between the rich array of parts and the whole? Does it welcome human engagement and occupation at all scales? Does it respond to its program and its technology in a way that not only accommodates but also celebrates its purposes?

So, let us start with the issue of an architectural story. There are, of course, many stories to be told about this building: the history of Scottish Parliaments, the decision to build a new building after the decision was made to devolve many powers from Westminster to Edinburgh in the late 1990's, the selection of a site among several options including the highly visible neo-classical Royal High School on Calton Hill, the winning by Enric Miralles of the competition to select the architect with a handful of hand-drawn sketches, the development of the design in the face of growing public anger about the escalating cost estimates from the initial 40 million pounds to an ultimate cost of ten times as much, the premature deaths of not only Enric Miralles on 3 July 2000 but also, only a few months later, of Donald Dewar, the leader of the client team—the former Scottish Secretary and then the First Minister of Scotland, the subsequent realisation of the building by the firm now led by Miralles' wife Benedetta Tagliabue in partnership with the Scottish architectural firm RMJM. But these are not the architectural stories told by the building.

And then there are the metaphorical stories told by Miralles as he secured the commission and developed the design. Stories about twigs and leaves, about upturned boats and fishes. Stories about the influence of paintings such as Sir Henry Raeburn's painting of the Reverend Robert Walker skating on Duddington Loch that was supposed to have helped shape important elements of the façades. These have all become part of the mythology of the building, as the public has attempted to come to terms with it and understand it. However these are not stories told by the building, they are stories told about the building.

So, what are the stories that we could learn from our experience of the building? It is a building of curves; walls curve, and roofs and ceilings curve. But the curves are neither segmental nor parabolic; at their centre they are segmental but before they could close, they extend in straight line tangents. The curves in plan are nearly always in opposition to each other, around a central

space, but meeting often at an acute angle. That this can also be a description of the edges of a leaf or a boat may be of some interest iconographically but that is not a sufficient reason for their existence.

Far more important architecturally is the role of the curve as it embraces and signals a space of gathering. This is a building devoted to bringing groups of individuals together, particularly in the Committee Rooms and the Debating Chamber, but also in smaller informal groups as in the Garden Lobby. The particular nature of these curves, that they do not close as in a circle or oval, has a more subtle implication. The circle, particularly, is finite. These gathering spaces are intended to be more open-ended and flexible. Jencks suggests that "Miralles evolved a gentle, more convivial curve. It opens up to the sides, so that conversation and consensus come before disagreement, at least architecturally. And Miralles provided each party with seats in the front row, and movable seating, to follow changes in political fortune."[6]

INTRICACY AND POETICS (TECTONIC CONSTRUCTION)

PL: Buildings are physically Intricate spatial settings, and also objects constructed of a multiplicity of parts, many of which could be considered alone, as necessary to the performance of the building, either structurally, environmentally, or functionally. However, Intricacy cannot be investigated simply in terms of a multiplicity of elements, but must be sought in their unity, I think, as a characteristic of a building's embodiment and embeddedness in the world.

JM: One of the most fascinating conditions of a building is during its construction, when many of its parts are still uncovered; but more often than not, as the building is completed, the vast majority of these components are concealed. A major reason for that concealment is that, like the mechanism of a watch or clock, most of the constructional elements of a building are regarded as having a servant role today, supporting but not participating in the cultural identity of a building.

This has not always been the case. There have been periods when construction was celebrated, although it has to be noted that there is usually some selective process at work that chooses some sub-systems rather than others (structural elements rather than drainage pipes, for example, although the recent HighTech movement includes them and airducts as well).

In the 19th and early 20th century the Arts and Crafts Movement in Britain celebrated the crafted materiality of buildings and the skills of those who made them. Pugin and Ruskin provided moral arguments that required an honest disclosure of both what a building is made of and of how it is made, and they were informed in their position by their admiration for Gothic architecture[7].

In Japan the architecture built under the influence of Zen Buddhism was committed to an aesthetic that valued basic constructional methods and a disclosure of the materials of construction. In the United States particularly, in the work of both Frank Lloyd Wright and the Greene brothers, these ideas from both Britain and Japan informed their designs. Another strand of thought, valued particularly by Wright, came from the French architect and theorist, Viollet le Duc, whose commitment to a rational architecture led inexorably to an effort to incorporate new materials and processes into his architectural language, albeit a language still much influenced by the Gothic Revival. Other followers of Viollet le Duc, such as Victor Horta in Belgium and Antonio Gaudi in Catalonia were more aesthetically convincing than Viollet in their efforts to derive a new architecture from his mode of thinking.[8]

When a careful examination of the Alberti designed façade of the Palazzo Rucellai revealed that the real constructional joints between the stones of the wall were not in the same place as the joints articulated architecturally on the façade it illustrated very clearly the distinction between the ideal order that much architecture intends to manifest and the pragmatic order that the exigencies of construction commonly generate.

PL: The Intricacy of the architecture is a phenomenon of its symbolic and tectonic logic, often derived from a tension between them, and from the architect's attempts to reconcile these two orders into an embodied and articulate spatial continuum between them. Architectural Intricacy might be summarised as paradoxically body and world[9], house and city, and as something capable of uniting the scale of an individual building with civic order (what Alberti called "civilitas"). Intricacy is not a matter of saying that a house should be like a city and vice versa (as critics tend to misinterpret Alberti's intentions), and it is not simply a matter of replicating things at different scales. Rather, Intricacy can work at the scale of a room, and in terms of the silhouette and armature of a façade. It entails judgements, and allows for hierarchy, makes visible the latent order and tacit meanings of a place.

JM: Throughout the history of architecture decoration and ornament allowed also for the elaboration of architectural form so that it might achieve a finer grain, a tangible human scale. The fluting on a "Dancing" Doric column at the Parthenon admits the human shoulder. The moulding around a door, or at the base of a column, is frequently graspable by the hand or embraces the fist, wrist, or forearm: the chair rail or dado is as conveniently located to the steadying hand as is the stair handrail; the base of a wall may be extended to form a bench height shelf; the fingers can explore the ornamented surface of a door handle; the eye lingers on the light and shade of dentils or the alternating roundness and sharpness of egg and dart carving. The senses of touch and sight are rewarded before the mind and the understanding are engaged. The human body is not only sheltered by architecture, it is encouraged to interact with it[10]. Niches may be created to frame that absence of a body, or in its sculptural equivalent; emptiness and silence.

It is interesting that in the 20th century the architects that became most creatively involved with the design of furniture, particularly chairs, whether Marcel Breuer, Gerrit Reitveld, Le Corbusier, Mies van der Rohe or Alvar Aalto (not to mention Eileen Gray and her architecture of screens), transferred to their furniture the need to physically engage the human body within their otherwise relatively un-ornamented buildings.

PL: Décor, as Dalibor Vesely observed[11], is not "mere decoration", or some sort of crime (as Adolf Loos suggested), but rather those aspects of spatial design which furnish the world. Intricacy, as an aspect of decorative ornament, articulates human situations, giving them dignity as well as comfort, and embodies, in a room, the spatial dimension of culture. Hans-Georg Gadamer insists that rather than extraneous or capricious, decorative ornament is intrinsic to architectural culture, just as architecture is intrinsic to culture itself:

"We have only to remember that the ornamental and decorative originally meant the beautiful as such. It is necessary to recover this ancient insight. Ornament or decoration is determined by its relation to what it decorates, to what carries it. It has no aesthetic import of its own that is thereafter limited by its relation to what it is decorating... Ornament is not primarily something by itself that is then applied to something else but belongs to the self-presentation of its wearer. Ornament too belongs to presentation. But presentation is an event of being; it is representation. An ornament, a decoration, a piece of sculpture set up in a chosen place are representative in the same sense that, say, the church where they are found is itself representative..."[12]

INTRICACY AND THE CLIENT'S PROGRAM

"I believe that the shapes of a building should indicate—perhaps display— the usage and way of life of its occupants, and it is therefore likely to be rich and varied in appearance, and its expression is unlikely to be simple."
—James Stirling

JM: Discussing his recently completed Leicester Engineering Building, completed in partnership with James Gowan in 1963, James Stirling argued that an architect should not only allow the different functions of a building to adopt forms appropriate to those different functions, but also that they have a responsibility to reveal them.

An examination of his design of the Leicester Engineering Building demonstrates that Stirling and Gowan set about achieving coherence by utilizing a consistent and limited palette of materials, colours, and geometric figures. The materials are red engineering bricks and red clay tiles, along with mass-produced pre-fabricated industrial glazing units. The repetitive geometric consistency of diagonal chamfering on the one hand distinguishes the programmatic elements of lecture theatres, workshop roofs and "Venturi

evacuation windows" from the laboratory wing, and from the corners of the office tower.

PL: Stirling suggested furthermore that this is a way to achieve diversity in a building's form, and thereby to avoid the banality of a "too simple unity". What he does not discuss in this instance however, is the requirement, which architects have inherited from Alberti's notion of "Concinitas", to achieve coherence in design. On the other hand, the architects achieved both unity in the extremely rhythmic repetition of geometric figures and constructional details. Identity and difference co-exist at the same time, as a result of the architects adhering rigorously to the logic of expressing (as individual built forms) each programmatic element of the overall composition. The result is an intriguing tension in the overall image of an extremely complex and yet laconic building, derived, I would suggest, from the Intricacy of its individual details and parts. The building rewards contemplation by making itself, and its program, legible and Intricate. It achieves a degree of Intricacy firstly by accepting the challenge of a differentiated program, and secondly by allowing that program to generate formal complexity. What is remarkable is that the architects are successful in disciplining that rhythmic and spatial complexity within a limited palette of materials, and in an asymmetrical, but paradoxically, balanced composition of the whole.[13]

JM: Aalto, an architect much admired by Stirling, relished the possibilities inherent in the architectural expression of a rich program, seeing this as a challenge to his creativity and, I would argue, as a source of potential architectural Intricacy. His design for the Town Hall complex at Saynatsalo (1949 competition, built 1952) comprised a series of everyday and civic programs: Council Chamber, Library, Offices, Retail and Guest Rooms, layered to create a microcosm of a city block.

PL: An allegory of an Italian Hill Town in fact, as Aalto put it in his competition report.[14]

JM: In this case Aalto's architecture Intricacy is derived from both program and detail. The site plan reveals that the complex is at the end of an echelon of other buildings, and the library wing is as much a member of that echelon as it is one of the sides of the courtyard that organizes the basic plan. Indeed, the library opens away from the courtyard towards the diagonal road that links the members of the echelon. The council chamber is uniquely on the second floor above the courtyard, and this extra height, plus the striking roof profile, gives it a dominance that anchors the composition. This roof profile is a version of the roof angles of all the members of the composition, thus part of a hierarchy of spaces, expressing the social hierarchy of the civic program, one nonetheless grounded in the quotidian aspects of the life of the town. The council chamber can be glimpsed through the gap into the courtyard that is oriented towards those other buildings. The gap is arrayed with an informal fan of terraces that contrast with the regular set of granite steps on the other side of the courtyard, adjacent to the council chamber. The formal steps are part of the primary entrance sequence to the complex, and to the courtyard, from which the major public uses are reached. Above the top of these steps is a pergola. The pergola has a similar rhythm to the fenestration that encloses the courtyard, but also orients the library outwards towards the courtyard and thus eventually towards the town, and the forest beyond. This fenestration is in contrast to the solid red brick walls that embrace the exterior of the complex.

PL: Intricacy here approaches a form of cultural literacy that is otherwise ordinarily absent in the blank walls and machine aesthetic of conventional modernist architecture. Intricacy is implied and is only fully revealed in use, over time. Intricacy is a function of the eye and the imagination I believe; it is characterised both by repetition and by rhythm, by hierarchies and similarities. Intricacy is an aspect of Being, it reveals the temporal dimension of human cognition and communication, the fundamentally spatial character of architecture, and its central role in revealing the embodied and experiential nature of human culture: Intricacy is existential. I don't mean that it is inspired by or inspires angst—the reverse in fact, it is lively, full of life. Intricacy in architecture is inspired by the Intricacy of the world. Intricacy in architecture is not a matter of style, it is not a characteristic of this or that epoch, it is a quality of mind, and of reflective thinking; it inspires and encourages reflection.

JM: Elsewhere in this volume is a discussion of the Schroeder house by Gerrit Rietveld where the interaction of the architect, his client, and their interpretation of the client's program, yielded a small building of great architectural Intricacy.

This page:
Town Hall complex at Saynatsalo by Alvar Aalto

Intricacy and Collaboration at the Schroeder House

John Meunier

Although there is no question that Gerrit Rietveld is the designer of this house, in that it bears the unmistakable imprint of a formal language developed by him in his previous work as a furniture and interior designer, it is also clear that this house stands out as an example of Intricacy—largely because of his client and collaborator, Madame Schroeder. It was she whose program for the house drove him into territory more daring and elaborate than was perhaps natural to him.

The house is famous for its second floor plan of moveable sliding partitions that offer a rich array of options between totally open or closed, between a set of individual spaces identified with specific uses and ownership, and a single large space with overlapping functions. That was Madame Schroeder's idea. The following are some quotations from an interview with her on 12 and 14 May 1982, three years before she died, having lived in the house and actively promoted the work of Gerrit Rietveld for over sixty years:

> "I think that in this house Rietveld isn't so completely 'Rietveld'. I think he adapted himself somewhat to what I wanted. And I believe I loved this house more than he did."

"So when Rietveld had made a sketch of the rooms, I asked, 'Can those walls go too?' To which he answered, 'With pleasure, away with those walls!' I can still hear myself asking, can those walls go, and that's how we ended with the one large space. But I was still looking for the possibility of also dividing up that space. That could be done with sliding partitions. I think that was an idea of Rietveld's, though he found it a shame."

"...he said once: 'It's really quite a nice house'. But it was too complicated, according to him, especially with the sliding partitions. He didn't even know how they worked... And he didn't really like all the admiration the house got; I mean, he wasn't particularly interested that it was so famous. Of course he was pleased that someone like Lissitzky admired it. And also that it provided him with openings to do more. But it wouldn't be true to say that Rietveld really basked in the fame of the house."

These do not appear to be the comments of a jealous client trying, as so often is the case, to claim that she really designed her house, and the architect was only a technician. Madame Schroeder was an enormous admirer of Rietveld ever since he transformed a room in the house where she lived, somewhat challengingly, with her older husband, remarking that, "It was a beautiful room, really beautiful, all different hues and shades of grey." Madame Schroeder talked about him as a good client will about their chosen architect: "I knew what I wanted, and it appealed to Rietveld straightaway. Only, he added to my ideas, he took them further."

What is important here is that the Intricacy of this house is borne from two sources: an extremely detailed and innovative program that generates a rich diversity of needs; and a highly resourceful but disciplined formal language, that remains coherent and consistent as it reacts to and finds ways to meet those needs at all scales; and then transcends them to create a convincing piece of architecture. The first came from Madame Schroeder, the client, the second from Gerrit Rietveld, the architect. It is notable, I would like to suggest,

that none of his subsequent work as
an architect achieved the same level
of Intricacy.

It is often noted that Rietveld
was first a furniture designer. While
it is true that he came from a family
of furniture manufacturers and
created some remarkable furniture
himself, he also received some
training as an architect and also as
a jewellery designer. In fact, rather
obviously considering his background,

Rietveld's first efforts at designing beyond the scale of furniture entailed the
design of jewellery shops. Nonetheless, it was as a furniture designer that
he developed the formal language, including the use of bold primary colour,
that he used, and elaborated, in the Schroeder house. Although the RedBlue
chair is his best-known chair, it is his Berlin Chair, arguably, that most clearly
anticipates the house.

However, the furniture not only provided a design language, it also
introduced other factors that affected his architecture. A piece of furniture
interacts directly with the human body, whether it occupies it, as a chair, or
manipulates it, as in the opening and closing drawers or doors. The design of a
piece of furniture entails creating defined and constructed spaces for human
needs. A piece of furniture is designed to welcome touch, as well as the eye;
it is dimensioned and scaled anthropometrically; it is often freestanding in
space and also articulates space, but it does so purposefully, meeting social
and/or practical needs; it is situational and situated. We will find that in
Madame Schroeder's house all these factors are repeated at both the scale
of the house, at the scale of a room, and at the scale of furniture.

One of the things that might first surprise a visitor to the house is the
almost naively frank and open way in which modern technical components

are integrated into its spaces. For example, components like the drain pipes (from the wash basins Madame Schroeder required in each bedroom); the water storage tank in her bedroom; the fuse boxes and the telephones on the stair half landing in the entrance hall; the speaking tube between the entry and the upper floor; the external rainwater pipes; a circular extract fan; a small ventilation and lighting window to the ground floor WC; wrought iron window stays, a cast iron stove and industrial metal radiators—all are left exposed. No attempt has been made to conceal them or contain them in a way that ensured that they did not conflict with the predominant planar formal language. That does not mean that the architect left it to the plumber or electrician to locate them: there is every evidence that both their selection and location were very carefully determined. Madame Schroeder tells us for example that:

"We thought central heating systems with vertical radiators were very ugly. Very much in the decorative style, it was all curly metal work at that time. Rietveld liked what we've got here very much; he chose it. The only thing we didn't know was that it would be so expensive. It turned out very complicated to install."

In the same way that a watch designer might leave the back of a watch transparent to show the way it works, revealing the Intricacy of its mechanism, by carefully revealing all of the workings of the house, Rietveld made it Intricate. In fact, in 1925 Rietveld designed and made for the Rademacher Schoner family, Utrecht acquaintances of Madame Schroeder and himself, a glass radio cabinet that revealed both the battery and all the components of a radio. A further example of this willingness to show how the house works is the simple hand lettered sign beside the front door. Pointing to the openable hatch where food deliveries might be made, alongside which is a hollowed out opening into a speaking tube, a circular opening is cut into the wall that echoes a rather larger and more visible circular opening for the extract fan at the upper level. Furniture, signage, equipment and ironmongery are integrated into the architecture— *are* the architecture. But these are not the primary reasons for which this small house has been widely recognised as one of the most important houses of the early modern period, and why it is exemplary of Intricacy in architecture.

A rich and inventive program, and the revelation of its operative components, while certainly contributory, needed to be integrated into a spatial and material composition that is both richly diverse and convincingly unified. In early sketches of the house it was a relatively simple box, its walls penetrated by rectilinear window openings, within which there were equally simple rectilinear rooms. There was one corner at the upper level eroded by wrap-around windows, and a simple canopy jutted out between the ground and upper floor on a half of one side. In the completed house nearly all the simplicity of basic volumetric form has gone. Only one room, the one on the ground floor that was originally intended to be a garage, retains its simple rectilinear shape.

All the other interior spaces are now much more complex: their bounding edges move in and out, or open up at higher level to reveal the ceiling of adjacent spaces. The movement in plan often accommodates built-in furniture or the impact of adjacent functions such as the central stairs or chimney core. Even the moveable partitions are not along straight lines as they create the upper level sub-spaces. In section too, spatial boundaries move as windows and walls advance or recede.

It could be claimed that the dissolution of spatial boundaries is simply a by-product of the decision by Rietveld to decompose the three exposed sides of the house, into a series of discrete rectilinear panels separated from each other both by colour and by spatial location; but that would be to undervalue the sense of pulsating energy at the edges of all these spaces, an energy that is ultimately released by openings to the outside. I'm thinking in particular of the dissolving corner beside the dining table on the upper floor: the rectilinear casement windows swing out at right angles, leaving the corner of the room and the house unmarked, and the interior space and the exterior space are merged.

Bertus Mulder, the architect who carefully restored the house in 1987 having at an earlier stage worked with Rietveld, identified "five areas of transition from outside to inside, or vice-versa. Four of these are horizontal, one on each of the three sides of the house and one on the eastern corner, and one vertical running through the centre of the house." Each of these consists of territories which both exist beyond and within the boundary of the interior. They are marked by balconies, patios, roof overhangs, wall extensions, supporting posts, doors (sometimes split in half so that the upper half might be open while the lower half remains closed) and, of course, by the outward swinging casement windows. The vertical transition is a glazed lantern alongside the chimney that extends the vertical volume of the central stair well above the roof surface. These transition areas allow the house to engage the exterior world, not simply by adding a porch or portico to a discrete box, but by applying to the periphery of the house the same sense of almost kinetic energy we find in the interior spatial order, and in the actual kinetic reality of the upper floor.

Compositionally the house is adamantly asymmetrical. This aesthetic characteristic, together with its scalar irregularity and asymmetric repetitiveness, might suggest that it could be said, in some ways at least, to exhibit certain aspects of the picturesque. One might suggest, that the picturesque is one aspect of Intricacy, at least in the sense described by John Macarthur. Macarthur claims that "The core of the picturesque idea..... is the aesthetic possibilities of the everyday world... seeking aesthetic value in the mundane and ubiquitous." He continues: "'uniformity'... is the enemy of the picturesque... 'intricacy', which is a visual texture and tonality the opposite of ..... smoothness; and 'variety', which opposes... 'uniformity.'" The picturesque, he suggests, is characterised by "its intricacy, its partial concealments, it excites that active curiosity which gives play to the mind". Picturesqueness concerns not the inflection of regular forms, he concludes, but a thorough "irregularity"; a concept of form based not on the symmetries of the human figure but on landscape.

Whilst each of the three exposed faces of Madame Schroeder's house are certainly asymmetrical and irregular, and different from the other two; each is carefully composed, and balanced. Unlike the architecture of Le Corbusier, there are here no regulating lines to impose a proportioning system that would guarantee a set of forms that shared the same ratios of width to height; so, in that sense, they are irregular rectilinear forms with a vertical emphasis, and there is one of these on each face, balanced by rectilinear forms of a horizontal emphasis. Vertical posts are balanced by horizontal beams or rails. The small vertical window to the WC on the ground floor has the small round extract fan opening as its reciprocal on the second floor. Irregularity is in equilibrium with repetition, establishing an intricate rhythm of components and pieces of equipment, inside and out. Arguably, the overriding spatial characteristic of the house might be described as a landscape made up of mutable territorial edges;

and its façades might be described primarily as exhibiting the characteristics of a field condition. Whether one wishes to emphasise the formal or spatial characteristics of the house aesthetically as picturesque, or spatially as layered and diverse, the various discrete components of the house are woven together into an Intricate whole.

In sum, one of the primary characteristics that we have identified as contributing to architectural Intricacy is the co-existence of a diversity of scales. These may range from things that engage the hand, to that which engages the community. Intricacy is not simply complexity, as I have noted elsewhere, but diversity that offers a consistent formal or architectural argument. Consistency is one of the most convincing aspects of the Schroeder House. Rietveld's architectural language—a language that is often associated with the De Stijl movement in general, is a highly disciplined language of rectilinear planes,

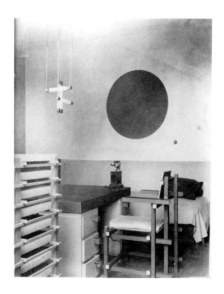

linear elements in strictly vertical or horizontal orientations, and a restricted palette of colours, black, white, grey, yellow, blue, red; operates at many different scales, from small scale furniture to walls, floors, roofs and ceilings, and is evident ultimately in the scale of the building as a whole. The fact that Rietveld honed his formal language in the design of furniture and then was able to expand it to the scale of architecture in this house is undoubtedly a major reason for its success. It is a language that allowed Rietveld to meet the needs of Madame Schroeder's complex and challenging program with wit and resourcefulness, whilst retaining a degree of irregularity and formal coherence: and it is a language that allowed him to respond to the larger cultural issues that were beginning to transform the field of architecture, literally and figuratively opening it to social and spatial Intricacy.

The Rietveld/Schroeder house in Utrecht demonstrates how significant, in the generation of Intricacy, are the challenges posed by a client when her demanding program pushes an architect out of their comfort zone. Madame Schroeder concludes:

"He did it, but he thought it was a pity.... He always regretted it, primarily I think because the space upstairs became considerably more complicated with the placing of partitions. You see it was like having your cake and eating it: yes and no. And Rietveld would have preferred: its either like this or like that."

The implication is that Rietveld liked neither ambiguity nor complication. But, arguably, these characteristics are frequently a source of the richness that, in the hands of a skillful architect, I suggest, can yield Intricacy.

I have argued elsewhere in this book that it is often ambiguous readings that generate Intricacy in minimalist work: complications elevate the artistic challenge to the generation of coherence; and it is this that distinguishes an Intricate work from a merely complex one.

The Schroeder House is a particularly interesting case, both because of its impact upon the development of architectural culture, and because no other work by Rietveld achieved such a level of recognition and fame. I would like to suggest that Madame Schroeder and her complex program played an important role in this cultural achievement and upon its influence on architects worldwide, but it is surely not the only case where client and programme were significant contributors. Abbé Suger is often given much credit for the rich and innovative programme of St. Denis, and I'm sure I could fill many pages with other examples.

The client and their programme are not the sole source of demands that an architect must attempt to satisfy of course, but they can, if an architect acknowledges their potential creative contribution, be catalytic towards the generation of Intricacy; and it is this that will intensify the quality of their work in artistic terms. This is a source of consolation as one recognises that whilst clients and programs are transient, and their buildings will normally outlast them, those works of architecture derived from Intricate relationships, will retain the qualities that inspired them.

At the Edge of
the Forest and a Field

Simon Henley

Buildings must be visited to be understood. You must be there. And do the things the architect imagined. At the very least move around, stand still and sit down. Take it in. Experience the space.

That is what I did, when, along with Patrick Lynch and David Evans, I went to visit John and Dorothy Meunier's house in the village of Caldecote outside Cambridge in the summer of 2019.

A few years before this I had visited Barry Gasson, John Meunier and Brit Andresen's Burrell Collection, a museum outside Glasgow, with my wife Claire: in both instances, being there, being with people—and the conversations that arise then and there—were all important in my experience of these buildings.

The Meunier House stands on high ground in an old orchard in the village of Caldecote, eight miles from Cambridge. It is relatively isolated but for a neighbouring house and the church on the other side of a quiet road, neither of which can be seen from the house. When we were there, the tough fletton brickwork intermittently reflected the warmth of the summer sun. John designed the house when he was in his twenties and teaching at Cambridge University. It was designed to be a family home, but also as a piece of research, exploiting economies in both space and construction; hence the use of the

common fletton. We arrived by car, first glimpsing the house through the branches of apple trees laden with fruit. Its apparent simplicity was masked by the infinite complexity of nature.

The house is constructed on a square brick base, the outer leaf of the brick cavity wall projecting two inches beyond the face of solid wall below. I couldn't take my eye off this sharp horizontal line. Such a simple idea, but one that reveals so well the architect's thinking: that ideas about the configuration and making of buildings should contribute to the profound pursuit of architecture. The construction of the Meunier House is elementary and so is the experience. The idea is abundantly clear; not diagrammatic in the way that a plan can be, but vivid in its relation to nature. No hyperbole, no distractions superimposed by abstracted architectural intent. Just building.

The plan, which overlays two squares, structures patterns of life: day and night uses; scales of spaces; and degrees of interiority and exposure to the

world. Here, their orchard, the Cambridgeshire countryside, and there a church spire on the horizon. Even in the lower volume and compact plan of the more enclosed bedroom interiors, the exposed brickwork suggests an unusually strong connection with the outside due to the raw nature of the construction. The living space, again shaped by the red fletton walls, is a larger volume, a scaled version of the smaller rooms. Brickwork and a light net of timber frames provide shelter. Tall glazed screens complete the tempered interior, whilst establishing spatial fluidity between the inside and outside.

Some 40 years later, John made an addition, again in fletton brickwork, to accommodate another bedroom and bathroom. Consistent in almost every way, it creates a backdrop to the original house, another context; and inside, through a doorway—which recalls the ones made at Chaco Canyon in New Mexico by the Anastasi Indians—opens up a new perspective on another world beyond the original north wall of the house.

Outside, the cubic forms of the original house shape two clay-tiled patios. The first of these, in the north-east corner, is approached via a causeway of gentle steps which emerge from the earth to which they belong. The patio is captured by two walls of the house, and by a third freestanding masonry block. This reveals itself from another angle to be the garden shed and bin store. The second patio, in the opposite corner, has a prospect of the orchard, its microclimate and vantage point the result both of configuring the house as such and positioning it in the top corner of the orchard.

Walking around the perimeter of the house, we discussed and touched the details: Architectural Brail. We sat amongst the trees, some way away from the house. We did, as I suggest, inhabit it. Later, we returned to the living room, via the second patio—another concrete stepping stone negotiating the realms of earth and acropolis, much like those leading up to the front door. There, around a timber table, both in the ambit of the house but also in the orchard, the conversation turned to the Burrell Collection and its architecture. One that is, like the Meunier House, a part of, not apart from, nature.

The Burrell was the subject of an international competition that Gasson Meunier Architects won in 1972. The museum opened twelve years later in 1983. In the intervening years Brit Andresen joined the design team and Meunier departed to the USA. So the idea is 48 years old. Which is odd. It seems to belong to our age, and to reflect many of our current concerns. Thoughtfully constructed, practical and ethical, it responds brilliantly in every respect to Sir William Burrell's collection of medieval stone doorways and windows, historic artefacts, paintings, tapestries and stained glass. Some of this can be gleaned from the drawings but much must be sensed.

Burrell was born in 1861 and died in 1958. Over a period of three quarters of a century he built up a collection of artefacts from ancient civilisations, late medieval and early Renaissance Europe; Chinese and Islamic art, and what was then contemporary late nineteenth century painting. In 1944 he donated the collection to the Glasgow Corporation, although he continued to acquire works and artefacts until his death. The bequest stipulated that the work should be housed in a new museum not less than 16 miles away from the city centre, and within 4 miles of the village of Killearn, itself 15 miles north of Glasgow, away from the pollution. But a site was not found during his lifetime, and not until eight years after his death when in 1966 the Pollock estate—although just 4 miles from the city centre—was donated to Glasgow Corporation. Today the estate is a park of fields and woods in which Pollock House and gardens, and the Burrell are set.

The competition was organised by the RIBA with four architects on the jury— Bill Howell, a partner in Howell Killick Partridge and Amis, Philip Dowson from Arup Associates, architect and writer Theo Crosby, and Jack Coia of Gillespie Kidd and Coia who, with Andy MacMillan and Izi Metzstein at the helm, had produced a now famous catalogue of buildings for the Catholic church, schools and universities many of which are in and around Glasgow. Bill Howell describes a process where the assessors developed the brief and judged the schemes.

The museum, like the house, was constructed in the corner of a field. In this case a decision that Gasson made during the first stage of the competition before he invited Meunier to join him for the second. The land rises to the north and is bounded by woodland on three sides and a road and avenue of trees on the south. The trapezoidal plan is nudged close to the trees, leaving as much as possible of the meadow intact. Its position on the edge suggests a certain humility on the part of the architect. From the main building, a long thin gallery extends to the road. This proboscis of sorts, with its gabled stone façade and medieval gateway salvaged from Hornby Castle for an entrance, marks the start of an extended threshold between the outside world and museum interior. Inside, this path removes the visitor from the "now" in which they first set eyes on the building to another dimension in time. The projecting entrance gallery also conceals the service road to the basement behind its west wall. But most importantly this sequence avoids any proximity to the building and its south elevation, relieving it of the more formal obligations of a museum façade. Instead the building swallows the visitor early, and takes them on a journey that spirals clockwise around the building's perimeter. The long entrance gallery ends in a top-lit court around which the reconstructed rooms from Sir William's former home—dining room to the south, drawing room to the north and hall to the east—are arranged. These are constructed in stone, and establish, along with the lecture theatre and temporary exhibition space, a band of monolithic buildings-in-miniature that bisect the plan.

The plan is simple, its logic derived from the organisation of the art and artefacts in relation to light. Stained and painted glass is exhibited in the brightly lit galleries behind the south façade. The stained glass is mounted above eye level immediately behind the fenestration at much the same height one might have expected to encounter it in its original setting, back lit and colourful. You must look up.

In the middle of the plan to the north of the lecture theatre and temporary exhibition space, in the darker parts of the building are the tapestries, protected from the sun. The rest of the museum is organised into a series of narrow north

south galleries that stretch from the tapestry gallery to the diagonal perimeter wall that forms the northern edge of the plan. Here, the enclosed galleries give way to an open space next to the woods.

One image in particular from the competition reveals the idea. It shows a short figure in front of a photograph of woodland divided into 8 vertical panels, although there is some ambiguity about whether it is portraying a single scene or multiple scenes of woodland. The image recalls Mies van der Rohe's use of the montage. These invariably used an image of a landscape, broken into vertical panels, the white space between each suggesting a mullion and as a result each panel to be a pane of glass. In front of this polyptych Mies would indicate internal space with a floor or ceiling grid and one or more elements within that space.

Mies van der Rohe's montage of the Resor House project in Wyoming from 1937 places a panoramic scene of mountains and treetops in the centre of the image. The photograph is again divided, in this case by two mullions, into a triptych and the photograph framed by lines to denote the window frame. In the foreground, corresponding with the two mullions are two columns. Mies uses their perspectival relationship to indicate first, there is space and that it is an

interior. Pedro Guedes, a young architectural assistant and Cambridge student, made a montage for the Burrell early in the design competition showing the proposed juxtaposition of the art work and its natural setting. Barry Gasson then made a similar image that follows a similar pattern, with the polyptych of a woodland setting. But where Mies depends on the frame and the columns to denote space, Gasson's image derives every aspect of the architecture from the placement of a single figure—below the base of the screen and left of centre—to convey the internal space. This single image represents a museum interior on the edge of a wood. In reality, the polyptych is translated into the north-facing glazed wall of the gallery. Outside are the woods; and inside is a field of artworks sat beneath a timber ceiling, supported by circular (tree-like?) concrete columns. Where the Resor House treats landscape as a picture, Burrell establishes the woodland landscape as an enclosure.

I walked on the edge of the forest and a field, following the glass, mesmerised by nature on the left, and artworks on my right. Nature and culture, not divorced by the architecture—as is the norm in a museum or gallery—but placed side by side: and I was in a reverie.

This page: Mies van der Rohe montage of Resor House
Opposite: Barry Gasson montage of the Burrell

Before lunch, when we were travelling up to meet John by train last summer, I was describing my visit to the Burrell to Paddy, and how it reminded me of walking with my dog on the edge of Parnholt Wood outside Winchester; walking in dappled light, beneath the tree canopy, but close to the open field. And this sensation proved not to be unique nor an accident in John's architecture, because he later talked of the idea that the museum would do just that: conjuring up an allegorical 'walk in the woods'.

Where one might normally expect to be removed from the world, exiled to the often strict geometries and axialities of a typical museum interior, the Burrell maintains contact with nature. This phenomenon stems from an experience that Meunier recounts from an early encounter with a Burrell artwork, how having been handed the piece by the curator it is explained it to them. Meunier recalls: 'That was the most perfect museum experience, and it has always lived with me as we have designed encounters with objects. The

closer one can get to that direct experience, the better.' He continued: 'In other words, the less we can put between the observer and the object, and also the more we were able to see the object in daylight, and in a natural setting, the better.' This is precisely what the Burrell does: illuminated by natural light, the artefacts are poised on the threshold with the natural world, the visitor too; mind and body are exposed to the art works and their architectural setting, unguarded and vulnerable; and as a result, we are more receptive to each artefact.

Gasson and Meunier invite us to inhabit the edge of their building, and in doing to inhabit the wood itself. The screen is the architecture. And, although it doesn't enfold space in the way that heavy masonry construction might, it adopts the space outside inside; conceives of the inside itself as a canopy— much like the wood outside.

The architects were determined that the timber ceiling should be uninterrupted by technology. They achieved this feat by locating the mechanical

Simon Henley

equipment—plant rooms and ductwork—underneath the gallery floor. This is combined with a series of stone-faced dividing walls within the gallery that route the services throughout the building. Their decision has meant that this highly serviced, complex public building, shares the elementary character of the earlier Meunier House. It also establishes a simple datum above which the public go, and below which they don't.

This organising device means that the galleries can be understood to be a plausible extension of the ground outside, and therefore part of the natural setting. Finally, the stone walls that "serve" these interiors can imitate the original masonry setting for the stone doorways and windows that Burrell collected and which the building preserves. Integrated into the new fabric, the ancient doorways and windows, instead of appearing to be curiosities in a modern building, are reabsorbed into it, and are (once again) a part of the architecture. It is, therefore, quite natural for the walls to serve as enclosures to "reconstructed" rooms. And, the ensemble—stone walls and free-standing stone-like columns, and glulam roof timbers—creates an appropriate setting for the stain glass fragments and for the tapestries in particular.

The glazed curtain wall itself is a timber structure, with close-centred posts above, and more widely spaced ones below a timber transom. The rhythm of the upper timbers intensifies the feeling of enclosure, something which is compatible with the closer rhythm of rafters overhead. Seen together, the mullions and rafters resonate with the rhythms of the trunks and branches of the trees, situated just beyond the glass curtain. The transoms give the building a corporeal scale, and the relative infrequency of the mullions below this element accentuates the transparency at eye level. Architectural experience is dynamic, unlike a photograph. The accordion of timber, the body's movement through it, the time of day, and the season: all play a part in the Intricacy, as Meunier would call it, of the architecture. As Meunier and Lynch suggest: "Intricacy is as much a temporal dimension as a physical characteristic of an art work, and fundamentally it reveals the primacy of the experiential character of art experience.'"

Leaving the building, I stopped and looked back at it. On arrival, it had consumed us so quickly, and so vivid was the interior, that only then did I take the time to consider its stainless steel and glass exterior. The materials and setting recall nineteenth century glasshouses, with their engineered unified enclosures; for example, Sefton Park Palm House in Liverpool (where Meunier studied at the University) and Kibble Palace Glasshouse in the Botanic Gardens in Glasgow, which both Gasson and Meunier would no doubt have visited. The association befits its parkland setting, but the precise formal type appears secondary: it is primarily a carapace for the collection, and your experience of it.

Whilst it's tempting to draw comparisons between aspects of John Meunier's work and that of others, it is the particular relation between inside and outside that these two buildings address. In particular, their response to the "type of site" that separates them from buildings that might for material reasons seem comparable. Colin St John Wilson and Alex Hardy's 1956-8 extension to the Cambridge School of Architecture, where Meunier taught for over a decade, arguably divorces the interior from the exterior. Whilst Bo and Wohlert's 1958 Louisiana art gallery in Denmark, like the Burrell, exploits the connection between gallery and nature, Louisiana meanders through a landscape exposing a variety of interiors to one condition after another. The resulting episodic plurality is quite the opposite of the singular nature of the Burrell's "walk in the woods", where the fabric of woodland becomes the substance of the architecture, and the morphologies of landscape compliment the intricacies of its interiors. It is the liminality that I experienced, in both the Meunier House and the Burrell, that distinguishes them from their contemporaries and antecedents. Today, the design of the Burrell is prescient, because it reminds us how façades help us attend to the natural world, as opposed to simply demarcating synthetic spaces set apart from it.

The Museum, and their current architect's decision (John MacAslan and Partners) to short circuit the entrance and to remove the reconstructed rooms from Sir William Burrell's Berwick-on-Tweed home (and the garden court that they surround); and to introduce a wide stair to the basement there, is blind

to the ideas of this building. The medieval gateway from Hornby Castle, and the journey that follows, serve to remove the visitor from one world; allowing the art, the artefacts and the building to reconnect one to the natural world, and to circular cosmic time. This quality of the building will be lost in MacAslan's project, or at least it will have to strain so hard to work due to the foreshortening of the original entrance experience (space and time to contemplate and to reflect will be sadly lost in the new accelerated arrival sequence that by-passes the original entrance). Fortunately, memory, photography and drawings will attest to the profound architectural intelligence of the original architecture. The "walk in the woods" will not be lost though and will remain, like our lunch in the orchard in Cambridgeshire, a powerful spatial experience. This quality is not just a matter of architectural form or the figure of a façade, or the representation of architecture through drawings and photography: rather, it is an aspect of building that can only be understood by being there: diurnal and seasonal time play a vital role, history and physical material, natural and artificial light, all play their part.

The Burrell and his house at Caldecote meet Meunier's own criteria (stated elsewhere in this volume) as a teacher for fine architecture: "the distinction that one might draw between run-of-the-mill buildings, and those that deserve to be called architecture, is that the latter reward contemplation; that the more one observes them, interacts with them, looks carefully at them and thinks about them, the more benefit one draws from them, both emotionally and intellectually."

Simon Henley

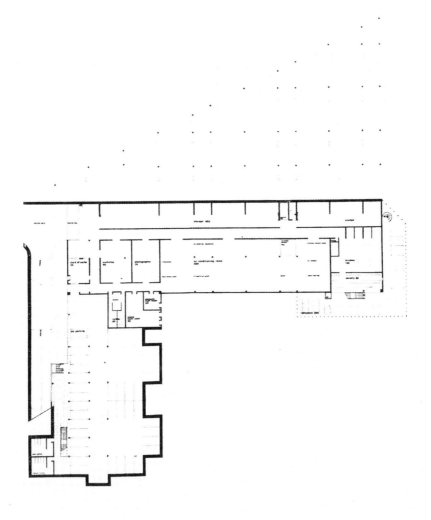

This page: Basement Plan
Opposite: Collage Site Plan

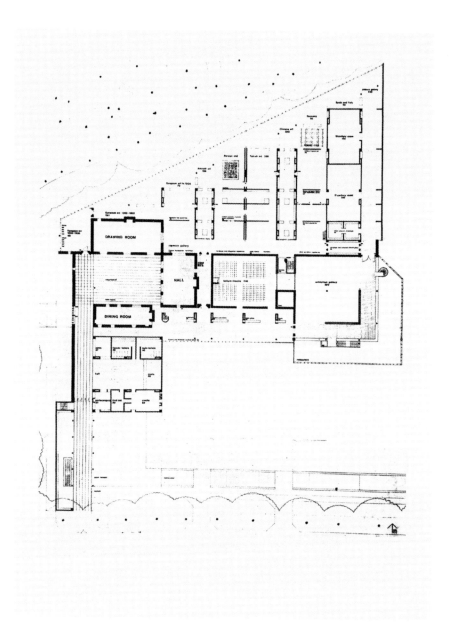

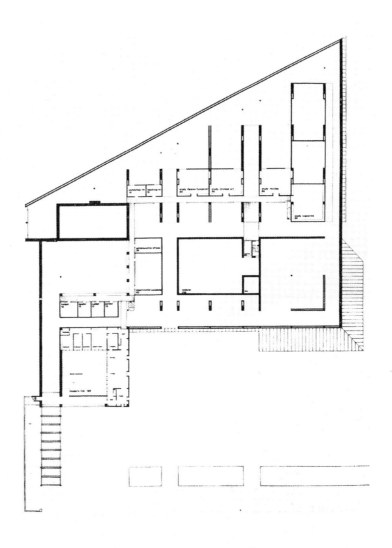

This page: First Floor Plan
Opposite: Ground Floor Plan

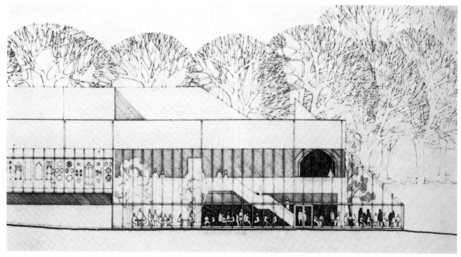

Simon Henley

Foothold

A conversation between John Meunier and Patrick Lynch, 2017-18

PL: I think that you are the missing link between a large number of famous British architects, and easily as good as most of them—indeed much a more talented and better designer than a lot of self-publicising polemicists from the late 1960s and early 70s.

    I can only understand your departure from this scene, emigrating to the US and becoming the head of an architecture school, (Director of Architecture and Interior Design at Cincinnati) and then Dean of the College of Architecture and Environmental Design at Arizona State University, as a love story of great optimism and hope.

JM: As one lives one's career, you never know the consequences of the choices one makes. I love making architecture, teaching and thinking about architecture, and the challenges of creative leadership within academia, but it has always been difficult to keep them in balance, particularly when faced with the other normal demands of family and community responsibility. We briefly discussed this while you were here. Cambridge had led me to believe that combining teaching and practice, including even academic leadership, was a reasonable option. Leslie Martin was an exemplar. But my move to the

States shifted the balance in favour of teaching and academic leadership, with only the occasional opportunity for practice—see attached my photos of the house I did in Cincinnati. But I have always thoroughly enjoyed the multiple chess game of the design studio where, as the instructor, one mentors the development of multiple designs and designers; and that has gone a long way to avoid my being a frustrated architect; and every now and then one has the pleasure of seeing something you have designed becoming a realised building or space. You will have seen the note I wrote to Ben [Derbyshire].

Email to Ben Derbyshire, President of RIBA, 10 July 2017
One of the many reasons that led me to give up my tenured position at Cambridge to go to Cincinnati in 1976 was because I saw some similarities between the co-operative education system that they were so successfully pursuing in Cincinnati and the so-called "thick-sandwich" system that the polytechnic architecture schools were following in the UK. I had been on several accreditation visits on behalf of the RIBA (I was on the Board of Education and Practice) and had developed some admiration and respect for that system.

In Cincinnati they had developed a highly sophisticated co-operative program where the students spent three months in practice alternating with three months in school from the second year through the fifth year of a six-year total professional degree program. Very importantly, students were paid during these eight quarters in practice, and the firms (the better firms from all over the United States and a few from abroad) vied to attract the best students, many of whom eventually joined these firms. In fact, some firms used the system to build their personnel. If you were interested I could fill in the details of the system.

I often tell the following story: When I was still a relatively new Director of Architecture and Interior Design at Cincinnati I met with a group of students to discuss their education. They were very frank and told me that they often felt that they learnt more during their three months in practice than they did during the three months in school. On reflection I concluded that this was not too surprising. In practice they were working on real-life projects with real-life architects, and getting paid. In school they were working on fictional projects with part-time architects and paying for the privilege; however much fun they were having. So I asked myself what to do, and came to the conclusion that the secret weapon of academia could, and should, be intellectual stimulus. And so I set about building a faculty of very bright young recent graduates from the better universities in the States. In fact, I hit one very productive seam of recent editors of Yale's *Perspecta* Magazine.

Architectural education, historically, was an apprenticeship system, occasionally augmented by some time either in a conservatory, university, or "club" like the Architectural Association. As it has developed, the academic component has become dominant, but with unfortunate consequences, particularly financial, for the students. Also, the emphasis on esoteric funded research within the universities in the UK has taken innovative architectural practitioners out of the ranks of full-time teachers. When I taught at Cambridge all the faculty, including me, Barry Gasson, and Brit Andresen, as well as Sandy Wilson and Leslie Martin were published practitioners, but that is no more.

So my sense is that we need to recover a richer relationship between education and practice. I was delighted to find myself discussing this with Patrick, and would be pleased to continue the conversation with you.

JM: Thank you for the great photographs you took of our home. I really enjoy your focus on telling details, and I recognise it now I have had the chance to review the book you left us on your own work. One of my working definitions of architecture is "buildings worthy of contemplation", and that is exactly what your photographs are doing, as, of course, it is what you are attempting in your own architecture.

PL: Perhaps it's a similar eye for how a tectonic joint can scale up to be part of a rhythm of a whole? Like you, I like very hard Architecture (and the Baroque)— sharp contrasts, volumetric situations, tectonic order, not just "space".

How important it is as that young lecturers build and built significant work? This would introduce the other topic of "cultured building" as pedagogy and administrative culture—as a form of creative organisation i.e. another manifestation of civic order? Alberti emphasises this in his Vita Civile and Della Familglia before he got to Architecture as humanism....

Current Burrell matters aside, can you remember how you went from small house projects to winning the competition? What was going on in your mind? What had you and Barry been discussing together and in the department?

JM: Houses were the starting point, and my own was a hugely important 'calling card' leading to the desirable situation when clients were not just looking for a young and malleable architect who could execute their wishes, but had some understanding of where one was coming from and would hire you because they liked and admired what you did (for example The Edington House and others followed on).

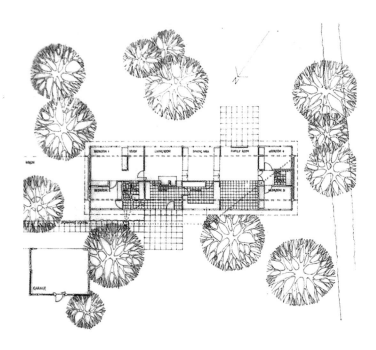

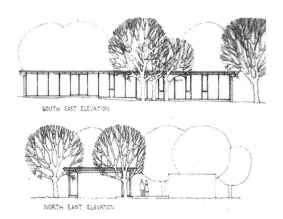

SOUTH EAST ELEVATION

NORTH EAST ELEVATION

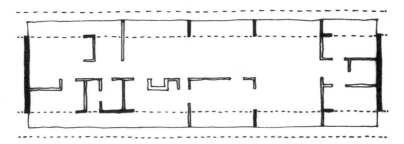

ROOF STRUCTURE SETS UP EDGE ZONES - AVOIDS MAJOR SPATIAL DIVISIONS

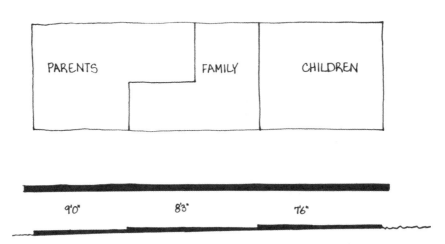

PARENTS

FAMILY

CHILDREN

9'0"   8'3"   7'6"

1'6" FALL ACROSS THE SITE USED TO GENERATE SCALE CHANGES RELATED TO BASIC PLAN ZONING

John Meunier and Patrick Lynch

From houses we graduated to relatively modest designs, and less modest studies, for academic institutions; notably several of the Cambridge Colleges such as Gonville and Caius, Trinity Hall and then eventually New Hall. Eventually we got out of Cambridge, and did an athletics pavilion for the University of Essex. While all this was going on, Barry's and my own academic paths diverged. We had both been hired on short term, five year, closed ended contracts. His was not renewed, whereas mine was, and I began to take on administrative responsibilities both within the school and within the profession (the RIBA Board of Education and Practice).

It was in that setting that Barry decided to take on the First Phase of the Burrell Competition, on his own, but then asked me to help with the final phases of the presentation. It was only for the Second Phase that we resumed our partnership with which we won that Second Phase. That, however, was not the end as the commission award was not automatic, and that was awarded to Gasson and Meunier, who had a portfolio and a track record, plus whatever status I had gained as a tenured faculty member at Cambridge. To be honest I cannot recall when Brit Andresen became a part of the team. I remained on the team until the end of Design Development when Barry and I parted company.

Barry and I had worked together for several years, as a compatible partnership, trying to do good and innovative work, building on each other's ideas. Barry's then wife, Liz, was an American artist, and that helped to sustain a relationship with fine art as well as a fresh eye. We obviously were affected by being in Cambridge working closely as academic colleagues with Leslie Martin, Peter Eisenman, and Sandy Wilson, plus all their interesting acquaintances. Both of us came from the North Midlands, me from Liverpool and the influence of Jim Stirling, Barry came from Birmingham. We had both studied in the States—Harvard and Columbia—and both worked for distinguished architects in New York—Breuer and Johnson.

I cannot say that we had long philosophical discussions about architecture, but retrospectively the one thing we shared was a commitment to the site and the programme, and a determination to find in them what Viollet le Duc called "A General Ruling Idea" as the architectural springboard for the building. That was the common denominator in all of our projects, at any scale, whether a house or the Burrell. On top of that were other issues like a strong geometric form, and a very direct and economical approach to materiality, construction and structure.

Obviously there was a lot going on in British architecture at the time, some of it very much affected by the USA (Eames) and of course the great giants, Le Corbusier, Mies and Aalto, but although I have to admit to being a great admirer of the Eames House and Aalto's Studio, we were not interested in emulation. Le Corbusier's *Modulor* and Wittkower's work on Renaissance proportional theory were important. I had stumbled on P.H. Scholfield's *Theory of Proportion in Architecture of 1958,* his MA Thesis at Liverpool, (recently republished), and found it eminently sensible and convincing as a way to secure the unity and diversity essential to good architecture. It had a big impact on the design of my house.

I had seen the *This is Tomorrow* exhibition of August 1956 at the Whitechapel Art Gallery, which had a great impact, particularly the Patio and Pavilion exhibit of Paolozzi and the Smithsons. Their idea of "dragging a rough poetry out of …" was particularly important, and certainly resonated with making an ambitious work of architecture out of common bricks not usually exposed to view. I could obviously go on and on, but let's stop there. Besides it's lunch-time.

PL: Yes, Stirling spoke about "organising the hierarchies of the program into a plan", and Rowe of course famously compared a "plan form" to a "diagram", thus dismissing Sao Paolo as a "built diagram" i.e. not architecture. Moneo makes a similar point about OMA, and Koolhaus "not being interested in design"; which I think is an allusion to "disegno", the Renaissance theory of architecture as order, what Alberti called "concinnitas".

It's a Liverpool trait, I think, to see the plan as a thing of beauty. And to try to reconcile geometric and structural order with a complex program into something that is something like a poetic economy of means.

I wonder if you know of Liam McCormick, another LSA alumnus? His churches in Donegal are exceptional, and like your work, exhibit exemplary control and compositional audacity. It's an unusual aesthetic, not Mies or Aalto, i.e. the usual antinomies, but an ascetic yet playful architecture operating within a strict sense of tectonic elegance, and a material sensuality derived from logic, or at least from a serious command of language and a sense of the game… Does this resonate?

JM: I was not familiar with Liam MacCormick though the plan for the Donegal Church does have an elegance I admire, if not the section and the roof.

You are correct that for me the elegantly resolved plan, probably a Liverpool thing, has enormous appeal; but I do not buy into the dismissive "diagram" argument. They are not the same thing, and I have always resisted "diagramming", that some instructors love as an intermediary to a plan. "Bubble diagrams" are dangerous, and for weak architects can too quickly become 'thin' plans.

I also insist that the section (plan) is often as important, or more important, as the ground plan. The clumsy layer-cake of the Donegal Church I do not admire at all, and I could not have ignored the interference of the columns with the sight lines. Irresponsible!

One person I forgot to mention is Christopher Alexander. We got to know him well when I was at Harvard. I worked with him and Serge Chermayeff, as well as Serge's son Peter, on *Community and Privacy; Towards a New Architecture of Humanism* during the summer of 1960. Chris was/is an extremely interesting person, the first typically Cambridge graduate that I got to know well; entering Cambridge with a scholarship in another intellectual field, and then bringing that discipline to architecture. Lionel March was another from whom I learned much. Both had backgrounds in mathematics, and the mathematical idea of an elegant resolution informs my thinking about 'good' plans.

From Chris I learned that you must start with the parts, and make them good first. Welding those parts into a good whole needs to be difficult, but should end up feeling inevitable. Start the design of a house with a good entrance, kitchen, bathroom, eating place, etc.; do not just fit them in.

PL: English landscapes: your work around Cambridge, in particular your own house, seems to me to be utterly rooted into the ground there. Where precisely did you grow up? Was the terrain similar?

JM: Delighted to get this note from you about picking up the dropped thread. So let me have a go at responding to your first questions.

I grew up in Southport, which is north of Liverpool, at the beginning of Morecombe Bay. The landscape in that area is very flat, not unlike the Fens north of Cambridge, but in Southport we talked about The Moss. But that flatness set up a delight in a more articulate and hilly landscape. I still recall with enormous pleasure my childhood summer holidays in the Lake District, and much later travelled in Greece with Scully's *The Earth the Temple and the Gods* tucked under my arm. So the site where we built our house is in the folded landscape of the Bourn Brook Valley with views across the valley, focusing on the village of Kingston as a picturesque piece of "borrowed landscape".

You are correct: the landscape was very important and the house was designed to incorporate it as an extension of the living areas. When we designed the house the original acre was an orchard with mostly a grid of old apple trees. We took out one line of the grid to open up the view from the living room. Wind and age have taken out many more trees over the 54 years of the house's existence, opening up much more of the distant views, and we were able to buy our next door neighbour's acre to extend the lot.

Brick, of course, is the material of Cambridge. The extension to Scroope Terrace designed by Sandy Wilson, which is where my office was, was not only built out of second-hand Cambridge brick but was also one of the major influences, along with quite a few other buildings, on my design. But I had a very tight budget (the house completed in 1965 cost less than £5,000 with me as the General Contractor) so I decided to use Common Flettons, made in Bedfordshire, as the cheapest brick.

John Meunier and Patrick Lynch

I was initially going to paint them but Barry Gasson's first wife Liz pointed out that they encompassed the Colour Palette of the floors and the ceilings and I was completely persuaded to leave them unpainted—one of the best decisions I made on the house.

PL: Thank you, that's a lovely description of your design process. Yes, the house feels very grounded, and of course your beautifully witty device of the barely articulated plinth delicately emphasises the joyful equilibrium between concept and materiality in the house. I disagree with Peter Eisenman's comment that it's a B+ project: understood as a whole, the integration of house and garden and extended landscape situates it very precisely in an English tradition of cultured domestic architecture. It's a highly tuned intellectual exercise I mean, but also very physical architecture.

In contrast, The Wendon House, the other house that you showed me last summer, arguably is a landscape, and is a premonition of much recent work (including Eisenman's) where the roof becomes a sort of extruded ground, the section all circulation, a "non-determinate landscape"? The whiteness emphasises its conceptual urgency perhaps? Can you speak a little bit about how the design evolved? It was your first collaboration with Barry Gasson, no?

JM: John Wendon, who was a local businessman married to an American wife with three kids, a boy and two girls, was directed to me by Sir Leslie Martin. He came to see my house and then invited me to be the architect. Barry Gasson had just joined the faculty and we had become friendly colleagues, so I invited him to collaborate as I have always enjoyed the experience of working with others.

Wendon had the license for an electric ceiling heating system—embedded wires in a plastic sheet that was pinned to the underside of the ceiling joists, radiating downwards. He wanted not only a family house but also to use it as a demonstration and advertisement for his system, so he was attracted to the idea of innovative form. He had purchased a lot on the edge of the old village of Barton, halfway between our house and Cambridge. Behind was an old

Opposite, top: Crit space in the extension of the Cambridge School of Architecture, Scroope Terrace by Sir Colin St John Wilson
Bottom: Noyes House in New Canaan, Connecticut designed by Eliot Noyes

Foothold   127

thatched cottage but adjacent were a row of developer houses of no great interest. This affected our decisions about siting the house, as did a few old apple trees that we felt could define an entrance drive.

The program included a relative novelty for English houses, but not American ones, a Family Room separate from a Living Room. We interpreted that as a space around which the children might gather, while the living room would be more for the parents and adult activities.

As you will gather I had become fascinated by Viollet le Duc, initially through the title essay in *Heavenly Mansions* by John Summerson and then by learning how important he was to Frank Lloyd Wright who claimed he was the only theoretical source an architect might need. He states that the key generating idea is not a preconception but must grow out of the careful consideration of the parts.

So we started with the living room and began to think of it as really a couple of connected spaces, one for communal gathering and the other for more individual private reading. These spaces might then have the slightly different scale, which might be leant by a change in level. This was the springboard for the key generating idea, which, after discussion with the clients, turned into a spiral ramp connecting many levels, culminating with a roof terrace with a view out over the old village. Obviously the Villa Savoie was somewhat in our minds. I had been to see it (in a dilapidated condition) on a trip to Paris in about 1954, which was also when I was able to visit the brand new Jaoul Houses, which was another influence on my own house. The ramp in the house is actually the same angle as the Villa Savoie, 1:6.

The design process was interactive with the clients. We would take our sketches mounted on boards to meetings with them and take them through our thinking, inviting them to participate.

Money was, as always, a critical factor and caused a fairly major rethinking of the built design. We worked closely with Davis, Belfield and Everest, Quantity Surveyors, who did a preliminary estimate on the cost of our initial design, which was not acceptable to our clients. So there were quite a few changes, including the loss of an external ramp—replaced by stairs—approach to the entry, which is in the middle of the sequence.

We were intrigued by Sandy Wilson's use of the White Forticrete Concrete blocks on his own house and office and decided to use them too, which introduced a new dimensional system. This time we used a brushed finish on the joints, as opposed to the bucket handle joint I had used on my house, as we were less interested in the individual block. Initially the house was not painted white but that became necessary as a part of solving a water leak problem caused by the pumped-in urethane foam insulation leaving bridging between the outer and the inner leaf. I think that the white over-paint has actually been an improvement as the Forticrete block eventually stains and grows mould, as you can see if you visit Sandy's house on the Grantchester Road today.

Much more to say but this is probably enough for now. On another occasion we might discuss my fascination with the geometry of squares.

PL: Yes, in both houses, and in your work in the states I think, geometric form, and its role in generating both a proportional system, and an overall macro and microcosmic sense of harmony, seems to be almost the essence of your architecture. You've already mentioned him, and I imagine that Wittkower's work on Palladio was incredibly interesting and exciting for your generation? And his student, Colin Rowe, was in the department at Cambridge, more or less directing Peter's PhD around this moment too, I think? Tell me more about your interest in squares. Did this evolve whilst you were in Marcel Breuer's Office in 1957, or as a master's student at Harvard? Did any of Colin's teaching at Liverpool (of Stirling and Maxwell et al) linger after his move south, and was his "mathematics" part of your education there?

JM: You are absolutely correct about Wittkower and Palladio, but I actually displaced Colin Rowe at Cambridge (taking over his lectureship in 1962) so I missed him then, although Peter Eisenman was still around finishing his doctoral thesis. When I was Director at Cincinnati we invited Rowe as a Visiting Professor for a few weeks and I got to know him well, but not at this point; but his *Mathematics of the Ideal Villa* was around.

Proportional theory was a big deal for me, as I said, and I later came across the book by Paul Scholfield, an alumnus of Liverpool, written in 1958 about the *Theory of Proportion in Architecture* that I found that I agreed with.

I gobbled up Le Corbusier's *Modulor* and was fascinated by the conjunction of Anthropomorphism and Anthropometrics but did not fall under the spell of the Golden Section. The square, with its ambiguity of primary and secondary axes, as well as the implied 45-degree axis was enough. I also, later, found myself just as fascinated by the root 2 rectangle (see the lecture). Scholfield did not fall for the magic numbers but saw that proportional systems were an answer to the challenge of reconciling the age-old problem of Unity and Diversity. I was also interested to discover that Le Corbusier did not invent regulating lines, which were well known in the 19th century, and a guy called Robinson had written a book on Architectural Composition in 1909 that showed how to use them, not only for organizing the rectangles in the elevations of the design but also by making them explicit with the roof angles. At Garches Le Corbusier did that with the angle of the exterior stair.

When I was a student at Liverpool there was very little discussion of proportion, even though Scholfield must have been writing his book at the same time. (My dates were 1953–7, 1958–9 with Breuer in the break). I'm sure that Dewi Prys Thomas, who taught theory must have covered it but it made no major impression on me then. It was also not a major subject of discussion at Breuer's. I guess it came to the fore for me when I went to Cambridge and found myself teaching First Year Studio and Theory when I argued that architectural form had three origins: use, technology, and the examination of form itself, beginning with the square/cube, and the circle/sphere/cylinder (good old Plato). I guess I never got beyond the rewards implicit in the square and its sense of resolution. (My Cincinnati house is a little more complex).

But you are absolutely correct in identifying a sense of harmony and resolution as the ultimate goal.

PL: Recent scholarship by David Leatherbarrow and Robert Tavernor suggests that the role of geometrical and proportional composition (lineamenti) in design, is always complimentary to the adjustments made by Palladio and Alberti of perspective, topography, decorum and use. I've written about the tension between ideal and actual architecture in *Civic Ground*. You've also been very interested in climate as well as topography, having lived and worked in the deserts of the American West. I'm very critical of Eisenman and Rowe for having confused design with drawing, and for ignoring the role of the sun's energy as an essential form of rhythm in architecture, not to mention the rhythms of everyday life, custom, habit, civic culture as festival, etc. Your work at The Burrell Collection seems to me to unite all these themes with another dimension of time, history. What's astonishing for me is how the building situates fragments from the history of architecture in relation to antique artefacts, placing a chronological narrative

in tension with Pollok Country Park, both its historic and natural setting. I love the audacious modesty of simply reusing things on the one hand (the archaic power of the entrance gable that you come across like a fragment of a dream); and then the frank confrontation of ancient objects and the verdant forest. I'm aware that this sounds wildly pretentious and sycophantic John, but the project reveals I think the analogical character of memory and imagination, and says as much about how we see the world as any cubist painting or philosophy of time. It's a profound contribution to culture, I mean. Can you say a little about the thought processes behind its creation, please? The quite complicated procurement and collaborative design process isn't that well known. I'm also very interested to know something about the intellectual climate that you and Barry et al we're operating in, what you were talking about, reading, etc.

JM: When I was a student at Harvard, 1959-60, I took a course with Siegfried Giedion, for whom I wrote an essay on the significance of the segmental curve in Le Corbusier's architecture and purist painting, and I cross-registered at MIT to take a course with Louis Mumford. Giedion's books *Space Time and Architecture* and *Mechanization Takes Command* were a big deal. He was in the Germanic tradition of seeing architecture as a manifestation of culture, a position I strongly hold.

After I took up my position at Cambridge in 1962 the book everyone was talking about was *Intentions in Architecture* by Christian Norberg-Schulz, a delightful man who came to visit us. He was a follower of Martin Heidegger and went on to write what was for us another influential book *Genius Loci: Towards a Phenomenology of Architecture*. The copy of *Intentions in Architecture* that is on my shelves I now discover originally belonged to Barry and I find that he wrote copious handwritten notes in the margins, so he clearly took it very seriously.

This is from the latter book's introduction:

"'Existential foothold' and 'dwelling' are synonyms, and 'dwelling', in an existential sense, is the purpose of architecture. Man dwells when he can orient himself within and identify himself with an environment, or, in short, when he experiences the environment as meaningful. Dwelling therefore implies something more than 'shelter'. It implies that the spaces where life occurs are places, in the true sense of the word. A place is a space which has a distinct character. Since ancient times the genius loci, or 'spirit of place', has been recognised as the concrete reality man has to come to terms with in his daily life. Architecture means to visualise the genius loci, and the task of the architect is to create meaningful places, whereby he helps man to dwell."

Another Scandinavian I found myself very influenced by was Steen Eiler Rasmussen, whose book *Experiencing Architecture* has been a constant presence in the bibliography for my Introductory Theory Courses, as I insist that the students must not only see architecture but experience it with all their senses and their minds.

I have always been very influenced by reading Vitruvius and Alberti and examining all the work that they spawned from Brunelleschi to Giulio Romano, Inigo Jones, and Vanbrugh. Historical buildings, including Gothic, Romanesque, Chinese, Japanese, and Islamic, as well as Renaissance, are still very much alive for me, and filled with lessons. Which is not to say that heroes of the modern movement, Aalto, Mies, Corbu, Rietveld, etc., and their successors, have not been my teachers.

There was a time when Jim Stirling seemed particularly interesting, the time when he built the Leicester Engineering Laboratories. It may have been Liverpool as a common denominator between us, or more likely the recognition that he had been looking hard at the British building stock of the 19th century. When I was a student at Liverpool we still did measured drawings, but Quentin Hughes had us measuring the cast iron and glass buildings of 19th century Liverpool.

The influence of Stirling might perhaps be seen in the Burrell. Glasgow has a lot in common with Liverpool as a west coast industrial port city that grew mightily in the 19th century. We definitely wanted Glasgow to be present in our building through all kinds of resonances. We also wanted the building to interact with the site, and let as much of the weak northern light in as was feasible, given the sensitivity to light of its contents. So the building faces south and north, with the sunshine passing through the stained glass, and the woodland to the north modifies the exposure to potentially damaging radiation. The juxtaposition of the art works with the woodland is vital to the character of the building and the experiences it offers, just as seeing stained glass against daylight and walking through ancient archways and gateways are critically engaging interactions.

PL: Finally, in both the houses that we visited together, and at The Burrell, experience of the architecture involves becoming exposed to much bigger scales of time i.e. the landscape, the natural world, etc. This experience is an intentional spatial narrative I think, designed to make one recognise and witness something specific—an existential (phenomenological?) architecture in fact, made up of moments, thresholds, pauses, changes of atmosphere, as you suggest. This "communicative movement" is why the plans by John McAslan + Partners for The Burrell, to create a new entrance, a "Hub" etc. in the centre of the plan, are so destructive. Whilst there would be minimal changes to the fabric of the building, the spatial sequence would fundamentally change, from a carefully calibrated encounter of historical artefacts in a natural setting, to a simply quantum increase in "space"?

JM: Two things are raised here: the notion of connection to the larger world both in space and in time; and the notion of structured sensory and intellectual experience as the goal of architecture. They are both very important to me. I am lucky enough to live close to Taliesin West and also to have had a long relationship with members of that community. Several

years ago I was asked to give a talk to the students there and I chose to pursue the argument that architecture was not just a question of intriguing (and photogenic) built forms, but rather an orchestrated set of meaningful experiences, and, of course I was able to use Taliesin itself as an exemplar. Those meaningful experiences need to be related to the rituals of life in that setting, and again I was able to refer to the rituals of the daily, weekly, and seasonal lives of those fortunate to live, or be invited as honoured visitors in that amazing place. More recently I was invited to participate in a symposium there by the new President of the School, Aaron Betsky, who was at one time a new teacher in Cincinnati when I was the Director. Although Taliesin West is barely a half-hour drive from my home I asked to be able to spend the night so that I could experience it around the clock, and as an honoured guest.

I should not go on about Taliesin West, although it has been a major enhancement to the architectural quality of my life in Arizona, but I am sure you know it well enough to recognise its relevance to the two issues raised.

This page:
Taliesin West by Frank Lloyd Wright

My first photo attachment is from where we currently live in Arizona where we have a daily reminder of ancient time and place with our view of Camelback Mountain, the reason we chose this modest little ranch house in the desert. The other attachments are simply to confirm what you have already recognised, that the Caldecote house is firmly nestled in its setting. We always guide people to it by telling them that our driveway is directly opposite the tower of St. Michael's 13th century church, which is next to a 19th century Vicarage that embraces a smaller medieval house.

One of the attachments is the early morning view from our Master Bedroom where you may be able to see the teapot that brings us morning tea in bed where we sit up and enjoy watching the sunlight wake the birds in our orchard; the ritual that starts our summer days. This note is going on too long but needless to say I find myself in strong agreement with you. The tragedy of the Burrell is a product of the architectural ignorance of the decision makers, and the lack of willingness by the architect to stand up to them.

Intricacy, Economy
and Invention

John Meunier

The Sports Pavilion at the newly built University of Essex was designed and constructed in the late 1960's. Barry Gasson and I won the commission as partners. The programme required changing rooms for men and women, plus a tearoom and bar. The site was in the middle of cricket fields and rugby pitches laid out in the grounds of Wivenhoe Park. The historic house is visible in one of the photographs. The three facilities, we decided, could be separated and grouped around an entry court, and we decided on an equilateral triangular grid (probably influenced by our enthusiasm for Frank Lloyd Wright's Hanna House). The changing rooms were necessarily introverted, while the tearoom and bar could be completely open and extroverted. We planned the latter to have room for two cricket teams to sit down for tea around long sets of diamond shaped tables, and there would be a central hexagonal bar around which the rugby teams could gather for beer after their games (we had played both sports, and understood their cultures).

We enjoyed the local red brick and, with purpose-made 120degree corner bricks, used them for the changing rooms. We decided, in contrast, to construct the tearoom and bar out of galvanized steel prefabricated window frames bolted together (celebrating the rhythm of the bolts) and stiffened by the bolted-on wood benches. Peter Dann was our very helpful structural engineer. We were very proud of the fact that there are only two different purpose-made steel columns, (one Y shaped in section, the other triangular and containing the wiring and switches for the ceiling lights), while the rest of the load is carried on the window frames. Note the exterior floodlighting; a lesson we had learnt from the Philip Johnson Glass House to stop the glass windows becoming internal black mirrors in the winter evenings (Barry had worked for Johnson).

The red Morgan in the photographs belonged to Barry and his wife Liz; we drove an old Ford Anglia. I am particularly fond of the photo with the children. They used the pavilion in the mornings as a day-care centre, which gave me a ridiculous amount of pleasure. The drawings came from my hand; I was trained in stoffage by my colleagues while working for Fred Angerer in Munich from 1960–62, and used the same techniques in my drawings for the first stage of The Burrell competition.

This economic but inventive attitude whereby the making of the building contributes to the architectural idea, the immersion in a landscape, and the resonance with the history of the pre-existing buildings in the context, are common to all of our work, both independently and as partners.

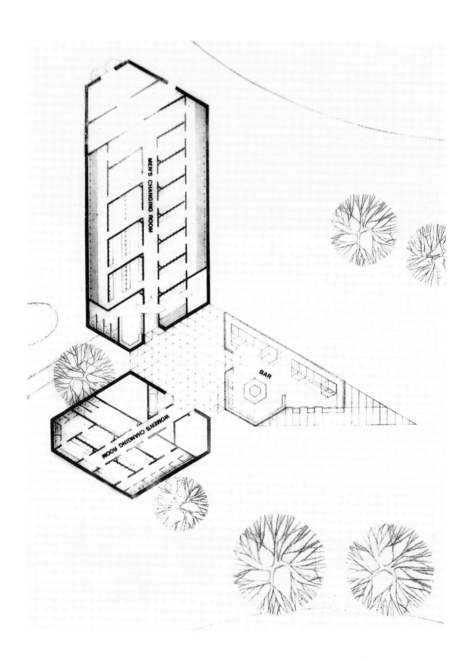

ELEVATION FROM SOUTHEAST CRICKET FIELD

UESP 3

ENTRY ELEVATION

UESP 4

The Lynne Gordon House
on Mount Adams in Cincinnati

John Meunier

In Cincinnati I was the Director of the School of Architecture and Interior Design. I had been recruited by the Dean of the College of Design, Architecture, Art, and Planning (DAAP), Bertram Berenson, (a relative of the great Art connoisseur) from Cambridge in 1976. He was both admired and well-connected in the Jewish intellectual community of Cincinnati, the home of Reform Judaism. He was also a very eligible middle-aged bachelor. One of his lady friends was a wealthy divorcee, Lynne Gordon, who fancied herself as an artist. As she developed her interest in him she asked him to design for her a house on a very prominent site on Mount Adams overlooking both the Ohio River valley and the downtown of the city, a thriving community since the late 18th century, often referred to as "The Queen City of the West" which was only displaced in its significance by Chicago at the end of the 19th century. Anthony Trollope's mother, Frances Trollope, lived and wrote there. The Taft family, whose grand 'white house' is in one the photographs, lived there at a time when one of them became President of the United States.

Berenson was more of a society figure than an architect so he asked me to help him, but quickly faded into the shadows leaving me in control and in direct contact with Lynne. I then discovered that the house she wanted at the time

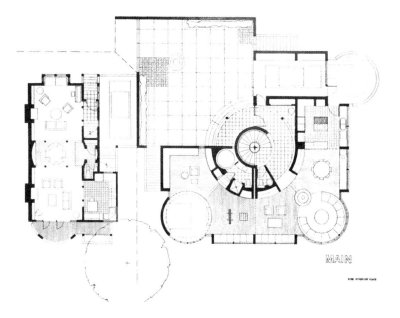

MAIN

was more a grand pent-house for a single woman than a full house with guest rooms, etc. (Sadly quite a few years later she did add a guest room with another architect that destroyed the house with a goiter-like protrusion below).

The site she had acquired offered extra-ordinary 270degree views. As well as the views the site was also very steep with a 50' drop, so the basic structure was a light steel armature reaching down to concrete short piles into the hillside. Around that steel armature we built a typical American wood frame house, with a double height living room on the corner commanding the central view through a tall window above a comfortable upholstered circular bench, and either side single height spaces, on one side the living dining room and on the other side a sleeping space with both a dressing area and closets, and a boudoir buffering the sleeping area from the living space, all enjoying the view.

On the uphill side of the house we created an entry courtyard leading to both a single-car garage and the entrance porch. In the center of the plan we built a gentle spiral stair that led up to a gallery overlooking the living area with access to roof decks above the lower spaces, and led down to mechanical systems and a store-room. The entry hall and circulation on one side filled the space between the stair and the kitchen/dining and on the other we built a bathroom and shower. One of the problems with a client from this section of society was that she insisted on employing an interior designer of her choice, which is why I offer few images of the interior, and also the reason I surmise that the house was not well published in the architectural journals.

This was the first building I had designed in a very visible urban setting where it clearly had some urban responsibilities. On most of our other projects the elevations and façades were somewhat secondary to the core ideas of the experiential relationships between the interiors and the surrounding landscapes. In an urban setting however the elevations and façades have to contribute to the culture of the city, as well as serve the purposes of the inhabitants. Civic propriety requires that the building address the community with decorum and contribute to its urban Intricacy. That is not to say that the building should not declare its own Intricacy but that it should do so in a way that it enriches the culture of the city.

I have written elsewhere that one of my civic tasks in Cincinnati was to chair its preservation society, The Miami Purchase Association (The Symmes Purchase, also known as the Miami Purchase, was an area of land totalling roughly 311,682 acres (487.003 sq mi) in what is now Hamilton, Butler, and Warren counties of south-western Ohio, purchased by Judge John Cleves Symmes of New Jersey in 1788 from the Continental Congress.—Wikipedia). In that role I was very interested in not only preserving the old but considering how the new should interact with the old.

It is in that context that this house was designed to acknowledge the ways in which, during its 19th century prime, buildings in Cincinnati had responded to conditions such as highly visible corner sites, linking two adjacent public façades with a circular bay. The house does not attempt to reproduce one of the traditional circular bays but is unashamed to acknowledge the precedent within

the context of a coherent modern work of architecture. It was not uncommon for those older circular bays to be elevated above a cast iron column; a relationship which also resonates with the elevation above steel columns of this house.

There is another resonance that I have enjoyed which was a by product of the decision to extend the central panels down to the ground with the casing of one of the structural columns that support the house. That decision was an aesthetic one but it reminded me strongly of the stick with which Venetian ladies held up their masks at a masked ball—reference perhaps to the modesty required of Lynne's private home in a very public setting.

The above aesthetic decision was made in the context of building study models of the house, an important design strategy that externalizes design ideas so that one can react to them emotionally as well as rationally.

Lastly it will be obvious that this house, designed nearly twenty years after the first houses, is still an homage to the square. But not without good reason.

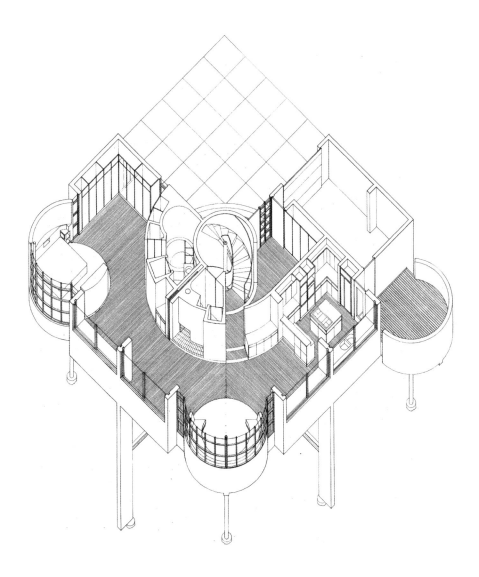

Intricate Labour

A conversation between John Meunier and Patrick Lynch
Spring–Summer 2019

PL: Can you tell me a little more about your childhood please? Your parent's occupation and their background? Meunier—French?

JM: The key issue was that my father, Stanislas Meunier, the son of a French born gas engineer in Stockport, was trained as a draftsman, although he made his living as a salesman of large-scale gas cooking equipment. During WW2 he designed kitchens for factories as it was government policy that everyone should have a proper meal for lunch where they worked. WW1 had shown that poor nutrition was very bad for the citizenry. My father brought these blue-prints home to work at the kitchen table. My father served the North West of England for John Wright Company.

   Although he wanted me to be an accountant I persuaded him that I should be an architect as I had shown in art classes at school that I had inherited some of his talent. I was also a fairly bright kid, had passed the 11-plus and was placed in the Transitus (fast track) classes at King George V Grammar School in Southport where we lived. My father had run away from boarding school when he was 14 and his disgusted older father, 50+ years old and in his second marriage, decided not to send him back to school and made him an apprentice in his offices. So, he had an incomplete education which he spent much of the rest of his life attempting to redress.

My mother came from a large family called Naylor. Her father, and his brother, made a fair bit of money building Bailey Bridges during WW1. As a young man he had gone to Pittsburgh to learn about the steel industry, and then returned to transform a smithy into a fabrication shop. Although my mother was trained in domestic science and cooking (she met my father when she was a cooking demonstrator in a John Wright Showroom) she was a strong proto-feminist. As the younger son with two older sisters I had no extra male privileges and was required to share in all the domestic tasks, including cooking.

It was with money that she inherited at the death of her father, that she supported me to sail to New York, from the fourth year at Liverpool, on a month's probation without pay, as an intern in Marcel Breuer's office. She was always more ambitious for her children than my father, who grew up being very careful with money. It was because of her that my older sister Ann went to the London School of Economics, and my other sister Lindsay went to London to be a dress designer. Both my sisters ended their careers teaching; Ann teaching Social Science, Lindsay as a dean at the University of Westminster in the Fashion Design department.

I owe my parents for my sense of optimism, and confidence, optimising whatever life may put in front of me.

As a follow up to my last note I have been thinking about what I learnt at King George V Grammar School that has influenced my work as a practicing and teaching architect.

From my art classes, very little apart from some drawing skills. The most influential teaching was by my English teacher, Mr. Paine, for whom I composed an essay every week, which he read and annotated carefully, and, if it was good enough, read out aloud to the class. From this I learned to form an idea and then to pursue it relentlessly.

Many years later I discovered the following in the work of Viollet le Duc (who was much admired by Frank Lloyd Wright) that rang a huge bell in my mind:

- When an Architect is called upon to erect a building, a confused scheme is probably laid before him—for written programs are generally such:—and it rests with him to bring these elementary instructions into something like order.

- Various requirements and services have to be provided for, and those must have his first and separate consideration: the architecture—that is to say the casing of these various services—must not yet be thought of: he will content himself for the present with simply putting everything in its place, he will observe in each part of the volume some chief point, and will give it importance, and thus his Intricate and complicated labour gradually becomes simplified (for simple ideas are the last to be reached).

- Then, having duly considered these several parts he endeavours to combine them, and again his task is one of simplification; but the ensemble of parts, simply connected, does not satisfy him; he feels that this body lacks unity; the junctions are apparent; they are awkward.

- He tries again; puts that on the right which was on the left; that in front that was previously behind; in fact he changes the disposition of his plan a hundred times.

- Then (I am supposing him to be a conscientious architect who loves his art and spares no pains to attain perfection) he reflects—laying aside the sheets covered with the results of his previous labour.

- Suddenly he thinks he perceives in his scheme a general ruling idea (observe, no one has suggested it to him beforehand).

- Light breaks in upon him. Instead of considering his design in detail, in order to plan the general arrangement, he reverses the process. He has gained a primary conception of the entire edifice, and of the way in which the various services should be subordinated to a simple and comprehensive arrangement then those details which had so much puzzled him take their natural place.

- The generating idea once found, the secondary ideas fall into their proper order, and present themselves when they are wanted.

- The architect has mastered his scheme; he has complete hold of it; he recomposes it in an orderly fashion; he completes and perfects it.

That is the core of how I design, but I recognised that it was also close to how I had been taught to compose an essay. They both need a generating ruling idea that is derived from a careful examination of the task and its context, which is then further articulated in a non-forced way. (Beware of the bed of Procrustes).

PL: I know exactly what you mean. My best teachers at school taught me English, and I did English Language and Literature A Level, which I loved. I still enjoy using the skills of Précis and Comprehension to structure an argument in composition. One of my prejudices against English architects in the main is the narrowness of the A Levels courses now, that people can give up history aged 13, and that someone at some time had the ridiculous idea that Maths and Art and Physics A Levels, without a humanities subject, are good preparation for studying architecture (some schools of architecture still request these A Levels... it's profoundly wrongheaded I fear). A lot of the problems of confused thinking and the inept use of metaphors in lieu of design arise directly from the lack of a basic secondary education, I believe. The tendency then to try to introduce students to advanced post-structuralist philosophy and linguistics at college... well, you know my views on the pernicious influence of Eisenman and co. His PhD was mostly an attempt to turn drawing into "analysis", confusing scientific code ie notation, with geometry, but geometry without any symbolic or cultural meaning: a mathematician's understanding of form, hokey metaphors, very literal, lacking in poetic nuance and contemplative critical distance, method but no truth, absolutely no wisdom. Dalibor used to enjoy pointing out that writing is a lot like designing, and I agree.

I was looking for background, but I wonder if we might not also include this dialogue? Why Liverpool University?

JM: My father originally thought that I should go into articles with a local architect, but he pointed out that Liverpool had a very good school of architecture and it was only a short train ride away. So my father took me to see Professor Gardner Medwyn and I started there when I was 17 in 1953. I commuted from my home in Southport until I left for New York, and Breuer's office in my 4th year. I stayed there an extra year, including a 3 month Vespa scooter tour of the States, before returning for my 5th year, this time based at 4 Mosley Hill Drive in Sexton Park.

It was the Beaux Arts tradition of 1st years helping on 5th year thesis projects that opened the Breuer door for me. I worked for Paul Castle, and he was in a house with Alan Cunningham, whose father was in Pilkington's Glass. Alan was about to go to Breuer's office for his practical training months, using the Pilkington connection, and I was able to persuade him to open the door for me a couple of years later. It was that experience that lead to Harvard and Munich and to Cambridge. Chance, opportunity, and bravado. The story of a career.

P.S. A couple of snaps from my Vespa Odyssey after I had spent a year with Breuer.

PL: Wow! Amazing… What did you learn on the trip?!

JM: The trip, first of all, taught me about self-sufficiency; finally being weaned to full, unprotected, adulthood. It also taught me that AIA awarded buildings were less interesting than the buildings recommended for visits by young architects in the offices.

John Meunier and Patrick Lynch

I was swept away by Wright when I visited the Hollyhock House in LA. Wright in my day as a student was not revered. That was the domain of Corbu, Mies, and maybe Aalto. Europeans were the thing, including the Russians and the Dutch. Eames managed to creep in via Mies in America and the Case Study houses as a kind of West Coast version of Mies.

But my emotional response to Wright took me completely by surprise. This was real architecture. Much later on I gave a lecture at Taliesin about Wright as a master of architecture, on the orchestration of experience, but the seeds were sown at that time.

The other things about the trip were the scale and the landscape, particularly as felt off the back of a 50 MpH max, unenclosed, Vespa motor scooter. I have this vivid memory of floating through a 70 mile wide valley, and then camping out in the open under a starry night sky with the smell of Ponderosa pines.

Further thoughts on grammar school. On reflection, as I said, I am not impressed by the teaching, apart from the English teachers, but I did get a great deal out of the extra-curricular activities. I was in three school plays, directed by another English teacher, acting as a woman in the first two (Maria in the School for Scandal wearing a dress designed and made by my sister Lindsay) and as Horatio—understudying Hamlet—in the last. I also played the clarinet—very badly—in the school orchestra. I was secretary of the debating society—where I developed some skills I was captain of the Colts (Juniors) rugby team, but was too small and light to play with the seniors. I was an off-spin bowler for my House cricket team and then later on a club team.

I took up club tennis after an experience in an intra-mural rugby game when I tried to tackle a rather taller and heavier friend on the other team, but bounced off when he put his hip into me. Besides, tennis was coeducational and I was 14 years old. I had my first date with Dotty seven years later on the tennis courts of Barnard College in New York, and we still play together. She only likes playing *with* me, not *against* because she thinks I'm too mean with my spin (remember off-spin bowling) and my drop shots, as well as my challenging serves.

I should mention that I did enjoy woodwork, and have since then designed and made a few tables in both of our homes. I know you could match, and probably exceed, all of the above, but they were all important to my development, and I'm grateful for them.

PL: Was your family ever religious? Did you know of Maguire and Murray's Work? And of Rudolf Schwarz?

JM: My family was not particularly religious. They flirted with Congregationalism but not too seriously. My older sister did marry an Anglican clergyman who had a late vocation from being an Oxford educated engineer, became an Industrial Chaplain, and ended up as Vicar in Epping. I have, however, always been fascinated by religious buildings of all denominations. One of the ways in which I know of Rudolf Schwarz and his generation of churches in Germany after WW2.

Religious buildings, and other buildings inspired by religion, inspire me because they embody value systems; and I certainly aspire to do that in my own work. As you may know one of my definitions of architecture is: buildings that frame and celebrate the rituals of life. Maguire and Murray were certainly familiar to me, but not in any way inspirational. I just thought that they did good work.

It's interesting that you should write today because I was just thinking of another short essay that I might write about my struggle to recognise that a good architect should not only do brand new buildings but also find a way to have a conversation with older buildings, both as neighbours and even within the same building. I did find that difficult, having been introduced to architecture at its Messiah phase.

When I found myself as President of the Miami Purchase Association for Historic Preservation in Cincinnati I invented a parable. I imagined myself as a newcomer joining a club or community that had been meeting for many years and enjoying a long-evolved discussion. The question was, how to act? Three options: to attempt to emulate them; to tell them to shut up as I brought the good news about a better alternative (the Messiah option); to listen carefully and then augment the conversation with my own ideas while respecting theirs. The first, of course is doomed to failure, the second too often the chosen course, and the third the more subtle and interesting. Out of all that came the Cincinnati House you already know, but not before I did a study of the way in which a gap in an older residential street might be repaired.

The other illustration of this effort would be the work I did on the house we live in here in Arizona, which is basically a 1959 building contractor's ranch house. We opened it up and took as a point of departure the rhythm of the steel windows, which I connected with that of the shoji screens that can close off the library/TV room to make it an extra guest room when needed. That room was originally almost completely separate from the rest of the house as what is called here a "man cave", that connects directly to the garage and the back yard.

PL: You seem to be unusually interested in context for a modern architect?

JM: Most of my earliest architectural mentors—Rietveld, Le Corbusier, Mies van der Rohe—seemed to even take delight in their work being radically different from the buildings in their context. And, indeed, they did embody forms, aesthetic concepts and technical realities that were in stark contrast to traditional architectural languages.

You will note that Alvar Aalto was not in that list, nor was Frank Lloyd Wright, not so much because I was not influenced by them, as because there are hints in their work (referred to in the attached talk) about their concern to respond to the urban context, Helsinki for Aalto and Venice for Wright. All of this to maybe help to explain some of the later developments in my work.

Certainly, one of the factors has been where I have lived since moving out of our Caldecote home. As you know we went from Cambridge to Cincinnati in 1976, where we spent 11 happy years living in a big old house in an area close to the University called Clifton. The house had been originally built in about 1830

in the middle of a relatively large estate, but in 1890 it was both enlarged and moved so that the land could be developed for some other quite grand houses.

We spent a great deal of our time in the round, domed, porch on the south-east corner. We did not live in all the house as we rented out (to pay the mortgage) a large apartment in half of the upper two floors. I know it's a bit of a stretch but you might be able to see some influence on the Mount Adams House I designed for Lynn Gordon.

The other house, in which we have lived since 1987 is the 1959 ranch house in the satellite town to Phoenix of Paradise Valley. We bought the house for its magnificent site. But that left us with too little money to build a new home, as we had originally planned. The original house was a quite modest typical American 1950's ranch house with quite simple boxy rooms, and so the challenge was to make a relatively few moves that would lend it some architectural spatial richness and coherence. The decision was made not to demolish the interior, but to draw from what was there.

First by simply opening it up to visually link the spaces, and then build on the rhythm and scale of the 1950's steel windows. The windows in the study provide the vertical rhythm for the book shelves as they did for the vertical and horizontal bars of the shoji screen between the extra guest room where the TV and the Library are. The Alvar Aalto furniture was originally bought for the Cincinnati House so it was as much of a given as was the original ranch house in Paradise Valley. The new wooden columns connect the furniture to this house as the beautiful wood floors did in Cincinnati. The construction on the wall was done by an Argentinian graduate student at Cincinnati to memorialise the Mount Adams House. For me the intertwining of the past and the present, the there and the here, is a source of great rewards. This really is enough.

Making Desert Cities

John Meunier

Modern desert cities, such as Phoenix, Albuquerque, Tucson, Las Vegas, even Riyadh and Dubai, are being made in ways that reflect the capacity of post-industrial technology to overwhelm the limitations that constrained the forms of older, pre-industrial, desert cities. It is debatable whether both the technology and the living patterns that typify such modern desert cities are sustainable. Some of the older desert cities have much to teach us about how to live well, without an excessive dependence on non-renewable resources, and without placing too much stress on the environment. At the same time, as Amos Rapoport and Besim Hakim have suggested, we must recognise that the forms in which cities are made respond as much, or more, to cultural imperatives, as to issues of climate and technology.¹ We need to be cautious, therefore, as we derive these lessons and attempt to apply them. Nonetheless, many of these older cities, such as Yazd in Iran, Shibam in Yemen, Jaisalmer in India, and Marrakesh in Morocco, have evolved in response to their desert contexts over extended periods of time. Some have even survived significant cultural shifts, such as in Sana'a in Yemen, with the arrival of Islam after many centuries of growth. It is argued that they may provide valuable models, regarding compact urban form, alternative house forms, climate control and its optimisation, water usage and its celebration, low-energy construction materials and methods, even the nature of windows, in the making of modern desert cities.

Desert cities in the United States, such as Phoenix or El Paso, even Los Angeles and San Diego, face a unique responsibility as they provide models for what it means to live a "modern" life in a desert environment. These models can multiply by many times the stresses placed on other ecological and political systems as they are emulated, partially or wholly, throughout the world—first by the wealthy in their suburban villas, and then, over time, by others in the population—abandoning the old dense city centres as they seek the benefits of a life that begins to match their images of twenty-first century urbanism.

In this essay (which was in fact originally published in 2007), I would like to address a growing concern by many regarding the long-term prospects of cities, such as the rapidly growing cities of the American Southwest, with both an urban form and an array of building types that have largely ignored their desert settings. It also is a response by the author based on extensive travel to desert cities around the world, particularly, but not solely, to older cities whose cores were built in a pre-industrial era, in search of lessons indicating more appropriate ways of living in a desert context. This work is not informed by nostalgia or cultural conservatism, although these are certainly forces staying the hands of those who would destroy, indeed in some places have already destroyed, the patrimony of ancient cultures in the name of "modernisation", and in response to the ineluctable forces of the marketplace. It is informed by a deep commitment to what Vitruvius called "propriety"; by a belief that the best way to live is not by dominating the context but by optimising its benefits and gently ameliorating its challenges; that the power of modern technology should be used only as a last resort when all other means cannot meet the demands of twenty-first century life.

DESERT CITIES

Top: City of Shibam in Yemen

Bottom: Housing expanding into the desert in Scottsdale, Arizona

BACKGROUND

The advent of twentieth century technology has radically changed the nature of desert city living in many parts of the world. Widespread use of automobiles, increased access to large scale urban water and sewage systems, almost universal access to electrical power and, in some cases, full climate control through air-conditioning have eroded the need for a careful relationship with both the social and physical environment. Satellite receivers, powered by that electricity, have infiltrated almost every household with images of ways of life that challenge indigenous cultural norms of both behaviour and artefacts. This barrage of images, reinforced by the communications from international commerce, has promoted the uses of the new technologies as a means to "modern" life patterns.

There are still many desert settlements in the world where access to all of these modern technologies is very limited. Automobility is at best a motorcycle, and much travel is done in mini-buses or shared taxis. Although electricity may be available via a tangle of overhead wires, water may be available only for a few hours a day or a few days a week, or has to be brought in containers from communal taps or wells. The building of sewer systems often has been less than satisfactory in some desert cities, as leaking pipes have both polluted the ground and dissolved the foundations of older buildings. Further, the effluent is often left untreated as it leaves the system. But these transitions to "modern" living, even when incomplete, have still been eroding ways of making desert cities that evolved over centuries and were adapted to the physical demands and opportunities of their physical and cultural contexts.

Is this process reversible? There have been political and religious leaders who have attempted to resist this tide of "modernisation". Countries such as North Yemen had rulers who refused to let their community participate in twentieth century developments throughout the first two thirds of that century. The resistance to this western model of modernisation may be reflected in some of the political turmoil in the world today among those who value the traditional ways of life and fear their destruction under the wheels of the juggernaut of western modernisation. However, even in countries that profess a cultural hostility to the west, many of the forces of "modernisation" seem to be irresistible. What is needed is an alternative model that retains much of what is valuable from the past but that also accommodates with a new sensibility the demands of the present.

MODERN DESERT CITIES

Greater Phoenix is a prototypical modern desert metropolis in the American Southwest. It is a city that anticipates achieving its full realization as a major urban centre in the twenty-first century and is accumulating the necessary elements of a metropolis. It is becoming a "major league" city more than simply in terms of sports. At the beginning of this century the population of the metropolitan area of Phoenix already had exceeded three and a half million, with a land area of more than twelve hundred square miles. The population by 2050 has been projected to be between nine and twenty-eight million, depending on which previous growth trend is extrapolated.[2] Phoenix has had most of its growth as an automobile city. As in other automobile dependent cities, its population density has been low, averaging about 2,750 people per square mile.

What could be the model for a different urban density in a desert city? Older American cities such as Boston, New York, and San Francisco have much higher densities and more urbane life-styles, and are among the most desirable places to live. But they are not desert cities.

I would like to conclude by looking for lessons in some successful desert cities in Israel, Iran, Tunisia, Morocco, Rajasthan, Egypt, Yemen, Australia, Chile and Peru. This is not a comprehensive array. Rather, it is a survey of a diverse set of long-enduring desert cities: each has its own lessons, not only at the urban scale, but also at the scale of the building types. Within the following brief survey, some shared characteristics may be identified. Among them are: shade; pedestrian scale and mass transit; courtyards; efficiency in water and energy use; natural ventilation and evaporative cooling; and enduring building materials; but most of all they share the characteristic of compactness (and Intricacy). A brief description of these characteristics follows.

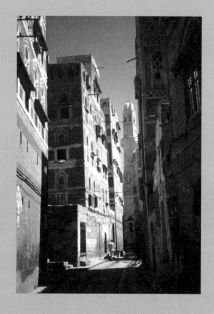

SHADE
Clockwise from top right:
Shade Structures in Brisbane, Australia;
Narrow shady street in Sana'a, Yemen;
Arcades onto the main plaza in Cuzco, Peru

SHADE

Shade is an essential component of desert living, particularly for the pedestrian. When one consults early photographs of the centres of cities like Phoenix, and of older Hispanic cities, porches and arcades (portales) are in front of almost every building, and awnings often shade the windows. In older cities in Australia, such as Adelaide, such "portales" are still to be found, somewhat like the cast-iron arcades of the French Quarter of New Orleans. In newer parts of cities such as Brisbane, high steel arcades have been constructed upon which shading plants climb. Major city streets are often lined with shade trees. Sometimes, as in Isfahan and Yazd in Iran, they are growing directly out of the irrigation ditches that flow alongside the sidewalks. In other North African desert cities, water is too scarce for all but the occasional street drinking fountain, often built as a philanthropic gift to the community by some well-to-do citizen. Here, the buildings themselves are the source of shade as they form the edges of the often-narrow pedestrian alleyways. In cities such as Shibam in the Hadramawt of South Yemen, the tower houses that line the street are so high that a great deal of shade is created, and the narrow city streets are noticeably cooler than the surrounding countryside.

Shade is particularly difficult to achieve at the scale of the typical automobile dominated street. The roadway is almost inevitably going to be exposed to long-term solar radiation and will itself become a radiant heat source. This can, of course be reduced by substantial shade trees along the sidewalks and in the medians, but such trees are rarely water conservative and would not meet the requirements for indigenous xeriscape plants often adopted by modern desert cities. This suggests that the higher density, pedestrian dominated parts of the desert city should be served not by streets predominantly conceived of as vehicular roadways with pedestrian sidewalks, but as relatively narrow shaded pedestrian ways, with limited access for service and emergency vehicles as well as purely local traffic. This is the arrangement for many of the streets of older desert cities. Physical conditions limit vehicular traffic to small service and public safety vehicles, or two-wheeled vehicles such as bicycles or mopeds. The widths of streets in the "medinas" of Morocco or Tunisia were often thought of in terms of the required number of laden donkeys or camels walking side-by-side. In a modern desert city, the dimensions could follow the minimums required for specially designed or selected essential vehicles, while recognizing the priority of the pedestrian, as do the malls on many of our university campuses.

PEDESTRIAN SCALE

Pedestrian scale creates a very different urban form than the scale of the automobile. Pedestrians need an intimacy of encounter with the environment, whether natural or man-made. They also need short-range destinations. This leads not only to a smaller scale environment but also to the possibility of a more varied geometry. Since the time of the 1785 Jeffersonian Land Ordinance that established a neo-classical subdivision of land west of the Appalachians the plans of most American cities have been dominated by the rectilinear mile-square grid. The interest in the picturesque that emerged in the mid-nineteenth century introduced the curvilinear street pattern, originally in our cemeteries and parks and eventually in our suburbs. The desert city, however, in providing for pedestrians, will often have an even more complex geometry in its pattern of major and minor streets. There are a few examples in history of desert cities planned for princes, such as Jaipur in Rajasthan, that are almost completely on a rectilinear grid, but the majority do not respond to a single dominant geometric concept.[3] This is not to suggest that they are illogical, but that the logic is not that of a simple geometry. Rather, as Besim Hakim and others have suggested, it is often the logic of religiously derived and legally enforced social relationships, and, as Norbert Schonauer has identified as worthy of emulation, the creation of a hierarchy in street networks linking small communities to the larger city.[4]

The dense network of intimate shady streets typically will lead to a major communal space. In the Hispanic colonial cities of South or North America, built under the influence of the Laws of the Indies, this will be a formal plaza, focused on a major fountain, flanked by arcades and framed by the buildings of government and religion.⁵ In Isfahan in Iran, there is an enormous central square, or "maidan", whereas in cities such as Marrakesh in Morocco the major open space (the Jemaa el-Fnaa) lacks such geometric clarity, but comes to life in the cooler evenings with food stalls and crowds clustering around story-tellers, snake charmers, tribal bands, acrobats, and even dentists. In most Islamic countries, formal geometry is reserved for the paradise gardens of palaces or mosques, not for urban spaces. Nonetheless, the central plaza is the focus of the community. The major Friday Mosque also will be nearby, and at dusk the air will be filled with the electronically amplified and distorted wail of the call to prayer (Adhan) from the loudspeakers mounted on its minaret. The vitality and identity of the city is relished by both its citizens and its visitors in such places. In the modern city similar public places are still necessary, and could relate to the transit systems that bring people from the further reaches of the city, thereby reducing the necessity for the major roads and parking garages that erode the intensity and thermal comfort of urban life in the desert.

In the ancient desert cities it is often from such places that the market, bazaar, or souk heads off as a shaded linear pedestrian passageway, burrowing its way through the fabric of the city. Typically this linear market will be flanked by occasionally fountained service courts, workshops and storerooms from which laden trolley carts head off to refill the emptying shelves of the small stores that line the pedestrian way, and also by the fondouks or inns that accommodate the visiting merchants. Bazaars or souks are often vaulted or domed, and illuminated and ventilated from oculi that let narrow shafts of sunlight in and the heated air out.⁶ Such spaces, neither interior nor exterior, shaded but open to the fresh air, are crucial to the success of desert city buildings. Whether such a form of retail would work in the modern world may be questioned but it certainly has its parallels in cities such as Scottsdale in Arizona that has a naturally day-lit, and in certain seasons naturally ventilated, shopping mall a half-mile long. The major difference is that the means of access via the automobile has isolated the modern mall from the rest of the city behind a moat of parking. With increased access provided by mass-transit, and a higher density of residences within walking distance, such physical isolation of shopping from the surrounding community can be significantly reduced.

COURTYARDS

Courtyards have been the focus of buildings in compact cities for millennia, but particularly in desert cities. The central courtyard allows the building to be constructed out to the very edges of its site, gaining most of the necessary light and air from within, rather than depending on a wasteful buffer around it of often relatively useless space. That courtyard becomes the focus of the building from which the major rooms are reached directly, and into which those rooms may generously open at cooler times of day or season. In very hot desert cities, as in Fez or Marrakesh in Morocco, the courtyard will have provision to be shaded when necessary with sheets of fabric stretched on ropes, or by open weave mats laid across a metal grille that protects the courtyard from invasion from above. Typically, within the courtyard there will be a fountain or pool and leafy plants that provide both physical and emotional cooling.

Buildings of this courtyard type were designed in the late 1950's for the campus of Arizona State University. The Farmer Education Building and the Social Science Building there have central fountains and planted courtyards around which the open-to-the- air circulation of the building, both stairs and galleries, is located. These stairs and galleries share the shade of the light mesh canopy over the courtyard. It is only on entering the rooms off that circulation that one experiences full mechanical climate control. The courtyard also becomes the major social focus for the inhabitants of the building. In some courtyards in Iran, for example in the desert city of Yazd, the pool in the courtyard may have a wooden platform straddling it on which a family and friends may gather in the evening to eat and converse. The courtyard will have on its southern edge, facing north, an open porch or iwan for use in the summer, and on its northern edge, facing south, a winter space, that in the nineteenth

COURTYARDS

Clockwise from top right:
Main plaza in Santiago, Chile; Wind tower and courtyard of the
Lari House in Yazd, Iran; Courtyard of the Social Sciences Building,
Arizona State University, Tempe, Arizona.

WATER

Clockwise from top left:
Water in the Atacama Desert leading to the oasis town
of Toconao in Chile; A monsoon tank in Rajasthan, India;
The town cistern at Hababa, Yemen

century may have been furnished with moveable windows glazed with coloured glass. The air movement through these courtyards and iwans is stimulated by windtowers, or baudgir, which climb above the rooftops and channel air from all directions down into the houses, iwans, and courtyards. In many older desert cities there is also space below ground to which people may retire in the heat of the day for rest, quiet, and contemplation.[7]

Such below ground space in Iran often surrounded a small pool through which the water from the qanats flowed. The qanats are underground channels hand-tunneled from the base of the distant mountains to bring water to the city. The residents of major institutions and the important houses of the city were served directly by these qanats. Others had to go to a communal cistern into which water would flow from the qanats. This space is covered by a dome and ventilated by an array of windtowers. Qanats are also found in North Africa, although there they are called khettaras.

WATER

Water is obviously crucial to the survival of desert cities. Many were built on rivers that brought the water from far beyond the sparsely precipitated desert context. Cairo is the most extreme example of this, but there are many other desert cities—such as Lima, in Peru, where the local rainfall is almost zero—but which are served by rivers fed from distant mountain watersheds. In the Chilean Atacama Desert, one of the driest in the world, there are richly vegetated fissures in the arid desert surface through which streams flow from the distant volcanic mountain ranges. Small oasis towns, such as Toconao, capture that water and guide it in narrow channels through their orchards, much as with the acequias in New Mexico and the great date palm groves of North Africa.

Another source of water has been groundwater in aquifers built up over millennia and replenished by seasonal rains. Sadly, in many ancient desert cities, such as Sana'a in North Yemen, the wells that almost every house had in its basement no longer reach the aquifer. This source of water has retreated beyond the reach of those wells because of profligate mechanical pumping caused by increased per capita use multiplied by rapid population growth. Water is now piped into Sana'a, as is the case in most of the smaller towns and villages of Yemen, where it is usually connected to communal taps in the street rather than directly to the houses.

In both ancient and contemporary desert cities, the modern technology of pumps and pipes, as well as canals that bring water from great distances, has changed patterns of water use as well as cultural attitudes towards water. The sense of water as a scarce and precious commodity, to be celebrated architecturally through noble fountains and the building of great cisterns and magnificent step-wells into which the monsoon rains are carefully channelled, can be seen in Yemen and Rajasthan. This sensibility has been displaced more recently by a purely utilitarian attitude that appears to have encouraged wastefulness. In beautiful old cities such as Jaisalmer in India, this newly excessive use of water overloads the inadequate drainage systems and erodes the foundations of older buildings that were not built to withstand the rising dampness.

In our modern desert cities there appears to be a growing consciousness of the need to be thoughtful about water. Many cities have adopted xeriscape as the standard for landscaping. Development also is constrained by the need to demonstrate the long- term availability of water, and an attempt is being made to avoid the exhaustion of the aquifers. In Phoenix, for example, the local press publishes articles about the loss of natural rivers because of the unconstrained increase in the number of wells within the watershed.

What techniques and attitudes can then be learned from the history and recent experiences of these desert cities? Water harvesting is a term that needs to be understood and embraced. Desert cities throughout history have practiced it. The modern desert city may harvest water at the scale of the watershed and the region but, at the scale of the individual building and the small community, many still have lessons to be learned. For example, throughout Australia many older homes have under their eaves a great round steel cistern into which the rainwater drains. It is used to relieve dependence on the main water supply in old mining towns such as White Cliffs or Coober Pedy, where many live in underground houses converted from the opal mines and harvest water from the ground above.

An older example is in the courtyard in the middle of the great mosque in Kairouan, Tunisia. Below the centre of the courtyard there is a cistern into which the rainwater that falls on that courtyard is drained, and is then available as a well for the ablutions required before prayer. At the centre of the beautiful small town of Hababa, also in Yemen, is the town cistern, surrounded by a wall of houses and a small mosque, into which the winter rains are drained and stored. In India water harvesting is now a requirement for all new developments. All other desert cities could benefit from such a fine grain attitude towards water conservation. The continuing use of water already used for ablutions is evident in Sana'a, the capital city of Yemen, as it irrigates gardens where fresh vegetables are grown. Here the Waqf, the local religious foundation, manages these gardens as well as the adjacent mosque.[8]

The celebration of water as a scarce and valuable commodity should be expressed in civic and private architecture, in urban form, and in management policies. As an example of what not to do; in a recent drought in Phoenix, the fountains were left dry to symbolise a commitment not to waste water, but this was actually misguided. The savings were negligible as the water used in the fountains is recirculated and the only slight loss would be through evaporation. Historically, fountains have been used to provide respite from the arid heat of the desert and to honour the cleansing and life-giving power of water. To keep the fountains flowing is to demonstrate the ability to continue life and civility in the desert. To turn them off is to admit defeat. The lesson here is in the appropriate use of civic architecture to celebrate the value of water as it is harvested and enjoyed.

ENDURING BUILDING MATERIALS

Earth is the material most used in the construction of many of the older desert cities. Adobe and rammed earth, or pise, often are dug from the immediately

ENDURING BUILDING MATERIALS
Clockwise from top:
Rammed earth Rick Joy Studio
Rammed earth construction in Morocco
Shutters below clerestory windows in Sana'a Yemen

adjacent land. From the North African settlements of Morocco, Algeria, and Tunisia to most of the Middle East the communities are made of it. The towered city of Shibam in Yemen, for example, is built of mud brick from the great wash of the Hadramawt.[9] Local stone also is used, as in Rajasthan, India, where the indigenous sandstone is extraordinarily versatile and can be used for columns, beams, floor slabs, as well as Intricately carved screens and brackets.[10] In Jerusalem, the city benefits from the continuing commitment to the use of its beautiful locally quarried Jerusalem stone on all of its buildings, giving a consistency and coherence lacking in many modern cities.

In some contemporary American desert cities, many architects of the Southwest have been exploring the use of rammed earth, adobe, and other more enduring materials and techniques that extend their palette to make a thoroughly modern architecture that fits their context as well as the contemporary needs of their clients. Eddie Jones in Phoenix and Rick Joy in Tucson are two of a rapidly growing school of regional architects whose work is being recognised far beyond the bounds of the region, and who have incorporated rammed earth as a valuable contribution to their architectural resources. Inorganic materials, such as earth and metals, that will not deteriorate under the fierce attack of sunlight and dry air have replaced wood as a primary raw material for the structure, or as cladding on the exteriors of buildings. Even the great wooden beams at Taliesin West have now been replaced by steel. In the arid air of the desert steel often can be left unpainted in the knowledge that the rusting process will be extraordinarily slow. Will Bruder has been a leader in exploring the use of metals, and his Phoenix Library is sheathed in locally mined copper that has been corrugated by the same machines that mould the steel sheets that form the walls of agricultural silos.

NATURAL VENTILATION

Air in the desert has been one its greatest assets. Many very talented people, such as New Mexico's great architect John Gaw Meem, as well as Frank Lloyd Wright, who located his Taliesin West in Scottsdale, Arizona, came to the desert to benefit from the clear dry air as a part of a treatment for their lung based illnesses. For many months of the year fresh desert air can be allowed to circulate freely through the buildings. The great mosques in the older desert cities of the Middle East are open to the air, without glazed windows. Indeed there is one mosque type that is little more than great arched porches, or iwans, on the four sides of an open fountained courtyard. In the older desert cities, there are many fresh-air environments where architecture is used to create exterior microclimates rather than closed interior environments. These courtyards, kiosks, porches, shaded souks or bazaars, gardens, or naturally ventilated major rooms, often domed and even fountained, lend much of the quality and richness to the fabric of older desert cities, particularly those of ancient Persia, Egypt, and the Arab world.

Some modern desert-based architects, such as Antoine Predock, have understood the continuing value of these architectural elements as they build in Arizona, New Mexico and other arid regions. Taliesin West, the winter home of Frank Lloyd Wright and his Fellowship, also had no glazed windows in its early years; just shutters that could be closed to keep out the wind or the cold night air. Similarly, older desert homes in the Yemen also had shutters only in their lower windows, with the higher windows "glazed" with thin sheets of alabaster to diffuse light into the rooms. High-level ventilation through lantern vents, or simply holes in the roof similar to that of the Pantheon in Rome, have ensured the evacuation of hot air from both major halls and linear vaulted souks or bazaars throughout the history of architecture in arid lands.

In the Islamic city, because of Koranic laws against overlooking into the private courtyards of neighbouring houses, there is a consistent height for all the houses. This permits a continuous stream of breezes above the rooftops. The wind towers of Iran, such as in the great desert city of Yazd, reach into that stream to play an important part in stimulating air movement within the courtyard houses, both through scooping air down on the positive pressure side of the tower and through drawing air out on the negative pressure side.

ENERGY USE

Fire or the naked flame, the source of light and heat for millennia in the desert as elsewhere, has been replaced almost entirely by the captured flame of electricity and by the ignition of fossil fuels in the internal combustion engines. Before industrialisation, it was the naked flame that cooked our food and heated us in winter, even provided the focus of social life. For example, in Aboriginal communities in the Australian deserts, fire, rather than buildings, marked human settlements. The acrid smell and smoke of cooking over charcoal or smoldering dried dung, has now been joined in the developing world by the choking exhaust fumes of mopeds, motor bicycles, taxis, trucks and trains. In these ancient sites, as in the developed world, the exhausts from the captured flame in engines and power stations have created a blanket of polluted air over our desert cities, particularly in winter when the colder night air causes temperature inversions that trap the dirty air. Efforts to control this have included a decision by the Indian Supreme Court in Delhi to mandate the use of Compressed Natural Gas (CNG), as the fuel for all public vehicles, including taxis and motorised rickshaws. Unfortunately, the decision was made before there were adequate refuelling stations, so long lines formed overnight at the few stations that did exist. Emission standards in the West have been constantly improved, more recently in the United States by states such as California rather than by a Federal Government sensitive to the objections of the automobile manufacturers.

Most encouraging as a response to this problem is a revival of interest in, and a commitment to, a new generation of mass transit. Many American cities are investing heavily, with the support of the Federal Government, in light-rail systems. Desert cities such as Phoenix are late to participate, and other smaller desert cities such as Tucson and Scottsdale, are still debating the value of such a commitment. Tucson, however, does have some of remnants of an older trolley car system to form the basis for such a network. Desert cities in the American Southwest owe most of their growth to the technological developments of the latter half of the twentieth century, notably domestic air-conditioning and the improved availability of automobiles. The density that results from automobile dependency is typically very low. Phoenix's density in 2000 was about 2,750 people per square mile. This density is about half of the density of Los Angeles, a city that developed initially as a trolley car city.

Other desert cities, such as Tucson and Albuquerque, have an even lower density. It is those low densities that make such cities appear to be inappropriate for mass transit. In Phoenix, in 2007 as this is written, there is an anticipated shortage of parking spaces, particularly shaded parking spaces, on the lots planned around the park-and-ride stations on the light rail system that is being built with a first phase planned for completion in 2008. Park-and-ride may be an appropriate way for mass-transit to serve a low-density city. An alternative, though, is to deliberately set about increasing the density around the light-rail stations in order to bring significant numbers of people within walking distance.

The construction of the 23 miles of the first phase of a light-rail system is one of the most important developments in Phoenix in the 21st century. A further 27 mile section of the light rail system, Phase II, is being planned. The fulfillment of the potential of this system depends on a radical change of urban density along those lines.

The system being planned for Phoenix, as of 2007, will total approximately fifty miles. If, for example, a density of 20,000 people per square mile could be achieved in a mile wide swathe centred on the light rail stations, then many benefits would accrue. First, the equivalent of a decade's worth of population growth, i.e. about 1 million people, could be accommodated, with a minimum of new roads and without consuming more land. Second, at that density not only would the light-rail stops be within walking distance of a significant number of people, they would also be equivalently close to almost all the other institutions of urban life such as schools, shops, libraries, post offices, restaurants, parks, community gardens, day care and senior citizen centres, etc. A density comparable to substantial portions of New York City could be accommodated along that strip, without sprawling the city of Phoenix (at present densities, another 364 square miles). It would reduce the amount of new road construction and automobile travel time that a typical area of Phoenix requires, and also restrain the increase in the air pollution that plagues the city. Such a strategy would have major benefits both for Phoenix, and serve as a model for other desert cities.

COMPACT URBAN FORM

What form should higher density urban living take in a 21st century desert city? High and low-rise condominiums currently being built, particularly close to existing centres with an array of services available within walking distance, follow models established in San Diego and Dallas. For some people in the urban area, notably young professionals and older people without children, this may be an appropriate although relatively expensive housing type. Higher density traditional houses also are being built. The open space around many of these houses, though, has shrunk to a margin measured in feet rather than yards. This limits the use of the open-air space that is one of the rewards of desert living where, for much of the year, it is possible and enjoyable to be in appropriately positioned and shaded outdoor spaces connected to the house.

The older desert cities, built before the days of the automobile and air conditioning have much to teach us about ways to live comfortably and well at higher urban densities. The late Norbert Schonauer wrote in *6,000 Years of Housing*:

"In a world where no nation is wealthy enough to afford waste, the land-use efficiency of the oriental urban residential pattern is worthy of emulation in terms of both land use and energy conservation. This is not to say that the oriental urban environment should be duplicated, but merely that some of its urban design principles should be adopted, such as, for example, the hierarchical order in street networks that bring about a safe residential environment.

Moreover, planning small precincts for residential neighbourhoods without through traffic would afford a more intimate identity with the residential community. In addition, a compact urban development pattern with no waste space would result in reasonable walking distance to many community facilities and would create the population density required for efficient mass transportation systems. Finally, the courtyard concept would be applied successfully in the design of both single-family dwellings as well as multiple housing in which each dwelling would have some semblance of privacy and indeed also a 'well of heaven'."[11]

The following comparison illustrates the urban land-use efficiency Schonauer analysed. The typical North American suburb has 23% of its area devoted to public rights of way, 6% to driveways and garages, 17% to built-up area, and 54% to private yard space, much of it just a buffer between the houses and between the houses and the road. He compared this to several other urban patterns: Tunis, Medina, 9% public rights of way, 74% built-up area, 17% private courtyard space; Ahmedabad, Kadwa Pol, 18% public rights of way, 69% built-up area, 13% private courtyard space; Baghdad, 16% public rights of way, 72% built-up area, 12% private courtyard space. In these examples, instead of only one sixth of the land being used for dwelling, between two-thirds and three quarters of the land is in residential use, and that does not count the private open space, nearly all in the form of central courtyards that are an intrinsic part of the home. This makes it possible to achieve much higher densities without building high or losing contact with the ground. It also allows the use of building and paving areas to collect the runoff from rains and support the plants that can flourish in its courtyards and along its pedestrian ways.

This comparison does not mention the great value of the roof surface of the desert house. Typically flat, it is accessible and usable. Residents use it at night, under the clear desert sky, as a cool place for sleeping. In the early morning, with the appropriate shade from the early morning sun, it can be a delightful place for breakfast. In the winter, the gentler sun can be enjoyed directly. In the Islamic city, due to the strict rules about overlooking, the neighbouring houses will not block the distant views. This becomes a welcome contrast to the introversion of the rest of the house. Even without the rule of the Koran, such height limitations could be easily assured within the planning controls of the western world.

PAST AND FUTURE

Desert cities have been around since the beginnings of civilisation thousands of years ago. Largely due to the extraordinary technological changes of the last century and a half, modern life has alienated us from much of the evolved wisdom of those millennia of urban desert living, even for those who grew up within such ancient patterns. For many contemporary desert dwellers, the term "sustainability" has attached to it a question mark. It would seem appropriate as we confront an uncertain future, where the optimism of modernity is being tempered by our growing concerns about the price it is exacting on our natural and social environments, for us to reconsider our heritage, not as something to be discarded, but as a source of valuable concepts. The past is not to be copied, but to be used as a reservoir of societal wisdom.

IMPLICATIONS ON PLANNING AND DESIGN

For architects and urban designers it is always a necessity to explore in design the implications of any critical theory. As both an architect and a teacher this author has sought to have the above ideas inform much of the recent work of his students. As an illustration of some of their work, as shown overleaf, a quarter square mile of Central Phoenix, just north of the downtown core and adjacent to one of the new light-rail stations, has been examined as a site for compact, mixed use, urban development with a morphology based on an examination of older desert cities and their building types. Two very different geometries were explored. One arrangement stayed close to the rectilinear grid on which Phoenix grew from the middle of the nineteenth century, but explored the use of housing types from cities such as Lima, Jaipur, and Jerusalem. The other arrangement responded more to the desire lines of pedestrians as they headed to and from the light-rail station, much as in Islamic cities the Friday Mosques, like magnets that order "iron filings", shape the elements of the urban fabric around them. In this case both the low courtyard houses of North Africa and the tower houses of Yemen were used as departure points in the development of compact city housing types.

The methodology, borrowed from other educators such as Michael Dennis of MIT, was to superimpose initially a piece of an older desert city onto the site, in order to establish a sense of the Intricacy of their scale, and the richness and variety of their fabric, and then to morph it to meet the demands of modern American urban life. Clearly, the culture that informed the logic of the older city is quite different from that which would shape a modern American city, and so it was necessary to reinterpret the form. However, it made some sense to replace mosques with schools, palaces with major institutions such as university buildings, mosque gardens with community gardens, etc. Discussions with developers suggested that the retail system of bazaars or souks was actually quite transferable. A limited accommodation of cars was allowed, but the commitment was to the primacy of pedestrian movement, much as is to be found on most university campuses. The students also developed reinterpretations of court and tower houses for modern American living. These contemporary applications, though, retained a commitment to use low energy building materials, such as rammed earth, to the optimisation of the natural advantages of a desert climate for much of the year, and to the use of architecture rather than machinery as the primary means of ameliorating the impact of the hot summer sun.

This early set of studies, which has been followed by other similar investigations into custom courtyard houses with a floor area ratio (FAR) of 1, i.e. lot size equals house square footage, and mixed-use compact urbanism, suggest that there is some validity to the proposition that informs this essay, I believe; that there are lessons to be learnt from studying older desert cities as we attempt to develop more sustainable ways to make the desert cities of the future.

Originally published in: Understanding Sustainable Cities: Concepts, Cases, and Solutions, 2007

PAST AND FUTURE
Proposed compact city neighbourhoods in Phoenix, AZ
adjacent to the Roosevelt light-rail station

Extending Intricacy

John Meunier

When I was appointed to an assistant lectureship at Cambridge in 1962 I learnt
that Cambridge University had a policy to make available second mortgages up
to 100% of the estimated value of a home purchased by a new faculty member.
This made it possible for me, with limited resources, to design and build as the
general contractor, a new home. The University had also relaxed the minimal
distance from the centre of Cambridge within which faculty had to live, which
brought into play economical building sites in the nearby villages. An acre of
old orchard was found, nearly eight miles west from Cambridge, in the small
hamlet of Caldecote. An existing small chalet was removed from a place close
to the site selected for the new house, which was in the north/east corner of the
land, giving the opportunity to open the main living spaces, and outdoor terrace,
towards views to the south/west. The final concept of two intersecting cubic
volumes sitting on a square platform evolved from an initial idea of a terrace
embraced by an L-shaped plan, not unlike some of Frank Lloyd Wright's Usonian
houses. The forces of that evolution were: first a concern about entry into the
back corner of that L needing greater generosity of size and welcome; second a
search for strong formal clarity that recognised appropriately contrasting scales
between the open and generous living spaces, and the more intimate sleeping

spaces; third a search for simple, clear, and economical technical systems both of structure and services. The internal spatial budget was one thousand square feet.

The interior of the original house with its young architect was published in *The Observer* Sunday newspaper in the late 1960s, in an article about architects and their own homes. This house was built of Fletton common bricks, glass, and Columbian pine for five thousand pounds.

The original house, designed and built between 1962 and 1964, was a small but resolved work of architecture built within a very tight budget for a young, as yet childless, couple. We lived in it until we left for the States in 1976, by which time we had two children. We were fortunate enough to be able to retain

ownership of the house, but rented it out on short term leases, fully furnished, to visiting scholars at Cambridge University, so that we could return in the long vacation for, often quite brief, summer stays.

It became possible for us to use the house for longer periods after our occupations in the States became less time demanding in 2002, as I had given up my Deanship at Arizona, and my wife had retired from her job in the College of Education. At that time, it was decided to add a new master bedroom wing: not an easy design task, extending such a compact square plan. There was also a question of which architectural language should be used some forty years after the original design. After much deliberation it was decided to continue with

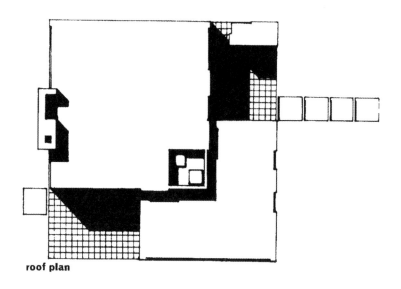

roof plan

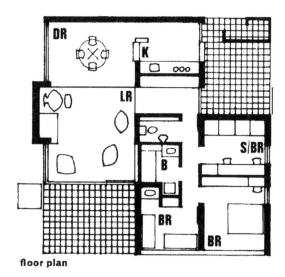

floor plan

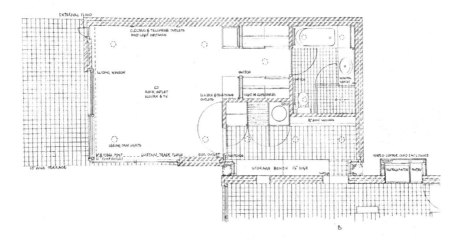

the original formal, material, and technical language. The extension is a double square sliding out from the north.

The decision was made to pierce the unbroken north wall of the original house at a point between the kitchen and the dining area, for an entrance to a gallery that would lead not only the new bedroom, but also provide some separation between the bedroom and the living area of the original house. A second penetration provides a peep-hole (much loved by grandchildren) from and to the gallery, and also announces the recurring thematic motif of a square, that pervades the old and the new structures.

The Gallery not only has a storage bench but also book shelves, a sound system, and closets that contain linens, a freezer, the electric circuit breakers, and a hot water storage cylinder. A structural column is located at the turning point and can be used handily to swing around.

There are a number of resonances between the new and the old parts of the house: the new master bedroom has the same dimensions, nominally 15' square and 10' high, as the living area in the original house; it is not just for sleeping, but acts also a more private sitting space that leads out to yet another

This page: Meunier House extension plan
Opposite: Meunier House plans

10' × 15' terrace, extending the "public parts" of the ground plane of the house into the garden. Brick panel walls add both more privacy and insulation, while also providing a parking place for the curtains—an outer blackout curtain and an inner translucent curtain. The smaller, slot window is narrow enough that it can be left open all night without risk of entry. The big openable window to the terrace has a lifting/sliding mechanism that locks down, like the sliding window in the original living space, that opens generously to the terrace, while also sealing against the outside air and rain when closed.

During a site visit it was noted that the brick work in the extension, particularly over the location of the bed, was not coherent, so it was decided to insert a square niche, similar in location and size to the peep-hole, which would not only distract the eye, but also provide a privileged location for flowers, or a valued object.

The extension connects to the original house with a recessed glazed slot that illuminates the gallery. The extension terrace repeats the terraces of the original house, linking the interior to the exterior and mediating the slopes of the orchard to the horizontal floor planes. The unbroken north wall of the original house is now re-established as the north wall of the extension, completing the cycle from windows in walls, walls in windows, to all-wall.

The openings from the living dining areas have enriched and extended the spatial experience within, augmenting the Intricacy and vitality of the house. The extension has resulted in the house further embracing and engaging the territory around it, including this in the Intricate life of the house, and of our extended family. Intricacy in architecture responds to Intricacy in life.

This page:
Meunier House before and after the extension

John Meunier

The Horizon of the Long Now

Patrick Lynch

"In general, facts do not explain values. And in works of the poetic imagination, values bear the mark of such novelty that everything related to the past, is lifeless beside them. All memory has to be reimagined. For we have in our memories microfilms that can only be read if they are lighted by the bright light of the imagination."
—Gaston Bachelard, *The Poetics of Space*

"It is well known that the primary meaning of proportion is analogical; and while analogy belongs to the metaphoricity of discourse, proportion more explicitly represents its structure, which can be eventually expressed in numbers. We do not need to be reminded that proportion was, until recently, at the center of thinking about architecture and its order. But it is not always understood or acknowledged that proportional thinking was primarily mediation between the ideas of a potential unity of the world and the uniqueness of a particular situation or phenomenon. In the history of Western culture, this process became a mediation between the celestial and the terrestrial order, between divine and human reality, and finally between the universal and particular in the understanding of the world."
—Dalibor Vesely, *Architecture in the Age of Divided Representation*

In his wonderful study of the alchemy of creativity, "Water and Dreams: An Essay on the Imagination of Matter" (1949), Gaston Bachelard drew a clear, and perhaps a somewhat didactic distinction between the formal and material imagination. Bachelard, who had begun his career as a historian and philosopher of science, developed into a formidable advocate of the primary importance of poetics. He believed that each aspect of the imagination, the formal and material, could be found in nature, and also in the mind.

The formal imagination in nature, Bachelard asserts, creates all of the unnecessary beauty it contains: the ephemeral beauty of snowflakes, the beauty of the orbits of the planets, the geometry of music and architecture, mathematics and rhythm. The formal imagination is expressed in the mind in a delight in novelty and surprise. The material imagination, in contrast, is found in nature as a characteristic of things that are primitive and eternal, and exists in the mind in an attraction to elements of gravity, weight and permanency.

It is tempting to see the different traits of the imagination[1] described by Bachelard as apogees of divergent cultural tendencies, antinomies even; aspects of antagonistic academic traditions (Formalism vs. Phenomenology?) between, and even within, certain Anglo-Saxon architecture schools; and to see them as symptomatic of a cultural war between theory and practise, one that seemingly refuses to be reconciled in a civic public discourse.[2]

INTRICACY AS RECONCILIATION

"I am convinced that the work of planners, architects, and designers is central to our cultures, for it is they who manifest and made concrete the values that inform our culture. But it is more than that, for as designers we can challenge, enrich, and elaborate those values. In particular, we can symbolize in our work the way in which our culture conceives of order. By ordering the human-made environment, we make it more accessible, more understandable, more supportive and more enriching. It is our job as educators to introduce our students to that task in a way that both challenges them and also leads them to the self-confidence they will need to be able to act free of dogma. They will need both technical knowledge and design skills, but most particularly and importantly we must put them in a position where they can act with cultural responsibility."

—John Meunier, "Cultural Responsibility, Design and Design Education: The Ordering of the Human-Made Environment" (Inaugural lecture as Dean of the College of Architecture and Environmental Design at Arizona State University, 25th September 1987)

John Meunier was appointed to an Assistant Lectureship at Cambridge University in 1962, succeeding Colin Rowe, who had left for Texas the previous year: Meunier's departure for Cincinnati in 1976, led (via Robin Middleton moving from the Architectural Association) to the appointment of Dalibor Vesely at Cambridge in 1979. Vesely and Rowe were friendly correspondents, and the latter is acknowledged and thanked in Vesely's magnum opus *Architecture in the Age of Divided Representation* (2004). Over this 40 year period the emphasis shifted within one single architecture department from a Formalist-Analytical approach to a Phenomenological-Hermeneutical one (which I learnt at Cambridge from Vesely and his colleague Peter Carl). John Meunier's period at Cambridge is book-ended by Rowe's and Vesely's time there, and whilst it is specious to suggest that architecture is solely the result of contemporary conditions; it might be said to be equally foolish to suggest that any academic or artistic discourse—like any "man"—evolves in island-like isolation from the flows and influences active upon it. In fact, Meunier recently described his house at Caldecote as "Palladian/Usonian/Brutalist"[3], and elsewhere in this volume he has insisted that his architecture demonstrates "the notion of connection to the larger world both in space and in time; and the notion of structured sensory and intellectual experience as the goal of architecture."[4] Arguably, the architectural imagination is neither solely formal nor material, and their reconciliation in creative design work is not so much a contradiction, as an inevitable paradox; beyond which lies "mediation between the celestial and the terrestrial order, between divine and human reality, and finally between the universal and particular in the understanding of the world." Vesely suggested that the imaginative unity of mathematics and metaphor in architecture, as analogy, traditionally offered hope, ultimately, for a "potential unity of the world"[5]. Such an ambition is obviously way beyond the scope and ambit of a short essay, and would perhaps be almost unbearably Intricate—as Intricate as a building, or anything else in the world. Nonetheless, it is clear I believe that Meunier's work as an architect-teacher sits precisely in-between the worlds of professional practise and academia; and he seeks I think, a unity of sorts. His work proceeds via integration of opposites, and Intricacy is, I would like to suggest, his word for their reconciliation.

FORMALISM AND MODERN ARCHITECTURE

"Proportional theory was a big deal for me, as I said, and I later came across the book by Paul Scholfield, an alumnus of Liverpool, written in 1958 about the Theory of Proportion in Architecture that I found that I agreed with."
—John Meunier, "Foothold"

The publication of Rudolf Wittkower's *Architectural Principles in the Age of Humanism* in 1949[6] had a profound effect upon Anglo-Saxon architectural culture, and arguably it still forms the basis of most design theory here. Wittkower's book is a curious combination. On the one hand, he introduced the idea that Renaissance architecture is the expression of a mode of philosophical thinking based on neo-Platonism, which he identifies as Humanism. On the other the book is distinguished by drawings that illustrate the author's "analysis". In line with the approach adopted by Jacob Burkhardt, Heinrich Wölfflin and Erwin Panofsky[7], Wittkower extrapolates from philosophy a theory of architecture based on supposed universal principles.

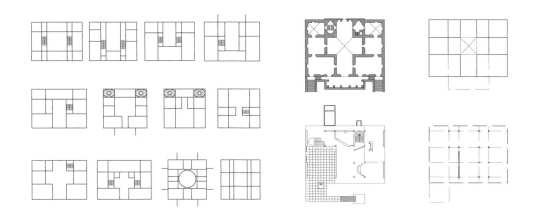

Most 19th and 20th art history in the German speaking world, in extreme contrast to the English tradition, derived its authority from philosophy and philology. So when this method is applied to architectural writing a theory of sorts emerges that sought to reveal the geometric "principles", or Platonic Form[8] lurking beneath the surface of buildings. This approach was demonstrated via drawings that radically reduce the plans that Palladio published in his treatise (which themselves show radically minimal information). Furthermore, analysis, in this method, consists of attempting to reveal rhythmic figures within the overall proportions of plan drawings, things that are not immediately obvious. Wittkower's argument that Palladio is a "Humanist" doesn't really stand up to scrutiny. Unlike his hero Alberti, who studied law at Padua University and held the chair in rhetoric at Florence University[9], Palladio did not attend a neo-Platonic academy (like Michelangelo) nor a university. What little he knew of antiquity was largely based on surveillance of ruins, but he knew very little about the actual intellectual principles that inspired classical architecture as an expression of Roman and Greek poetics and artistic theory. In particular, the symbolic aspects

Above, left to right: "Schematized plans of eleven of Palladio's villas", from Wittkower's Architectural Principles in the Age of Humanism; *Plan drawings of Palladio's Villa Foscari/La Malcontenta and Le Corbusier's Villa Stein, from Rowe's* The Mathematics of the Ideal Villa. *Redrawn by Lynch Architects.*

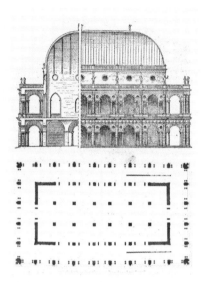

of classical culture are not really addressed by Palladio in the way that Alberti addresses questions of character and representation[10], and his treatise is not so much architectural theory as a sort of Users Manual or DIY guide to amateurs and would be patrons.[11] Its accessibility and lack of intellectual content (and lack of Albertian erudition) perhaps explains its popularity in Britain and America[12], and Alberti's relative obscurity here.

Wittkower perhaps chose to illustrate his arguments with the work of Palladio because of its popularity in England, and his readers' familiarity with it via various translations. Yet he not only over-stated the case for Palladio embodying the principles of humanist architecture; he also understated Palladio's actual contribution to architectural theory, by largely ignoring his written commentary and emphasis on the primary role of decorum in design. Furthermore, in reducing Palladio's buildings to overly simplistic diagrams, the situated character of their brilliance is lost, something that recent scholarship has emphatically sought to redress.[13]

Wittkower's famous student at The Warburg Institute, Colin Rowe, wrote a Masters dissertation in 1945, without any factual evidence, suggesting that Inigo Jones intended to publish an architectural treatise. The physical realm was clearly no hindrance to Rowe's fecund imagination, and he famously extrapolated on his teacher's methodology in his celebrated essay "The Mathematics of the Ideal Villa", which was first published in *The Architectural Review* in 1947. Whilst developing his own approach[14], Rowe's article might be said to be to some degree an attempt to show that Wittkower's approach could be applied to contemporary design, and he compared and contrasted the villas of Palladio and Le Corbusier, overlaying diagrams seeking to reveal the geometric principles exhibited in each. Rowe studied at, and then taught at, Liverpool before Cambridge; and his influence upon the former, alongside that of James Stirling and Peter Foggo (who also studied and taught at Liverpool[15]), was marked, establishing a "seriousness" in the school, Meunier suggests.[16]

Whilst we might find Wittkower and Rowe's approach (and Peter Eisenman's) to be outrageously reductive, and I have suggested such

Opposite:
Palazzo della Ragione, Vicenza, by Palladio, 1614. Note the variations in the column bays of the facade relatively to the inner, older structure.

The Horizon of the Long Now   233

elsewhere[17], in post-war Britain the idea that architecture exhibits principles that can be readily understood and integrated into modern design must have been extremely attractive and potent. Wittkower's writing style is pleasant, and his thesis is not too difficult to grasp: he has the gift of making you feel cleverer for having understood it. Architects are arguably preternaturally drawn to theories that can be communicated as drawings: Le Corbusier had established a modern publishing tradition of sorts by juxtaposing drawings and photographs in his various polemics. The fragments of modernist theory that Bauhaus exiles managed to bring to England were similarly revolutionary. In contrast to this, and to 19th century notions derived from painting and literature (The Sublime, The Picturesque, etc), Wittkower offered a sense that underlying the surface attractiveness of this or that style, architecture could communicate, in its own way, profound cultural ideas. To the nascent architects of the British Welfare State, recovering from global conflict, and recently returned from service overseas[18], the capacity for architecture to represent and to embody political and artistic ideals must have been irresistible.

John Meunier encountered a very rich architectural culture in the US, both initially as an intern in Marcel Breuer's office (1958-9) and then as a Masters student at Harvard (1959-60). Meunier attended lectures at both the GSD and at MIT, absorbing at source the ideas of Sigfried Gideon and Louis Mumford, and became intimate with Serge and Peter Chermayeff, and Christopher Alexander (who had begun his academic career as a mathematician). He observed that Gideon "was in the Germanic tradition of seeing architecture as a manifestation of culture", and confirmed to me that this "is a position that I strongly hold."[19] His interest in proportion, and in particular in the primacy of the square as the basis of compositional order (discussed elsewhere in this volume), underlies the plan form of The Meunier House and The Gordon House.

> "Colin St John Wilson thought of himself as reconciling Corb (especially his Maisons Jaoul) and Aalto. Similarly, Sandy's preferences in art were more iconographic and figural e.g Kitaj, than the Bauhaus-like patterns e.g. Ben Nicholson, favoured by Lionel March. Speaking of English modernism, Stirling's History Building—what might be termed English Constructivism—was won in 1963, the same year Leicester was completed; and of course the 1959 competition for Churchill College failed to select (Stirling Gowan's project) The Blenheim of the Fens... brick brutal carried nuances that reached from the rustic to English engineering via proportion, whereas concrete brutal was mostly about form."
> —Peter Carl, email to author, 27th November 2019

John Meunier arrived in Cambridge in 1962, a year after Rowe had left somewhat suddenly, sick it seems of the intellectual atmosphere at what that he later disparaged as "Fenland Tech"[20]. Meunier recalls the influence of Christian Norbert-Schulz on the department at Scroope Terrace, and also the nascent tradition of an English modernist architecture built out of indigenous materials which Leslie Martin (the professor and head of school) and Colin St John Wilson were developing in Cambridge; particularly the brick architecture of Harvey Court (built for Gonville and Ciaus College with Patrick Hodgkinson) and Wilson's houses on the Granchester Road and for Christopher Cornford, as well as his extension to the architecture department at Scroope Terrace. Wilson wrote well and published "close readings" of a number of projects by the Swedish architect Sigurd Lewerentz, and he attempted to describe an "Other Tradition" of modern architecture derived in part from the influence of the English Free School of William Butterfield and George Street.[21] Nonethless, the establishment of The Martin Centre as the research wing of the Department of Architecture by Sir Leslie Martin in 1967 (as the Centre for Land Use and Built Form Studies), under the directorship of the mathematician Lionel March, was

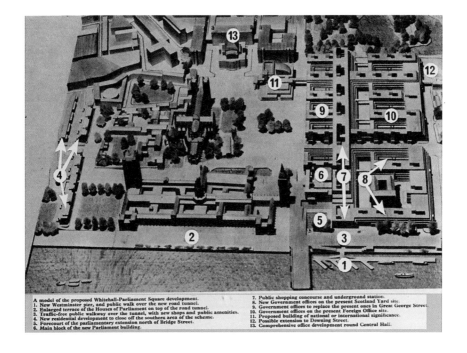

A model of the proposed Whitehall-Parliament Square development.
1. New Westminster pier, and public walk over the new road tunnel.
2. Enlarged terrace of the Houses of Parliament on top of the road tunnel.
3. Traffic-free public walkway over the tunnel, with new shops and public amenities.
4. New residential development to close off the southern area of the scheme.
5. Forecourt of the parliamentary extension north of Bridge Street.
6. Main block of the new Parliament building.
7. Public shopping concourse and underground station.
8. New Government offices on the present Scotland Yard site.
9. Government offices to replace the present ones in Great George Street.
10. Government offices on the present Foreign Office site.
11. Proposed building of national or international significance.
12. Possible extension to Downing Street.
13. Comprehensive office development round Central Hall.

stridently rationalist, and the intention was to establish a theoretical basis for the study of architecture, in particular at universities like Cambridge[22]. March published books on number in architecture[23] and his work emphasised the scientific basis for, and systematic character of architectural form[24]. He later held academic posts in "systems engineering" and "computational design" in the US, and was also involved with Martin in his aborted project Whitehall: a Plan for a National and Government Centre[25], which would have entailed demolishing The War Office and erecting in its place a concrete mega-structure with a series of square voids. March and Martin published a seminal essay, "The Grid as Generator" in 1972[26], emphasising the role of this in modern urban design. Rowe cannot simply be described as a formalist of course, and his interest in phenomenological philosophy is evident in his essay "Transparency: Literal and Phenomenal", written with Robert Slutzky in 1956. In other words, the influence of the thinking of Christian Norberg-Schulz[27] on the Cambridge school, suggested by Meunier above, meant that the formalistic analysis tendency of his friend Peter Eisenman, whose PhD, *The Formal basis of Modern Architecture*, Rowe mentored, and which grew out of the work at the Martin Centre; was tempered by an approach at Cambridge that emphasised spatiality and the rootedness of cultural meanings in architecture.[28]

Such was the intellectual firmament that Meunier was teaching in and designing in at Cambridge, that arguably his work of this period reflects the extreme tension between mathematical systematicism on the one hand, and a more nuanced material-tectonic-cultural sensibility on the other. The Meunier House arguably exhibits both tendencies at once, reconciling these apogees of thought into a satisfyingly simple and coherently Intricate whole. Arguably, it was in search of a unified synthesis of craft and theory that led to Meunier's departure from Cambridge University, towards the more apprenticeship-like method of architectural education that he found in Cincinnati.[29]

Perhaps most relevant to this story though, is the fact that it was expected that lecturers in the Department of Architecture at Cambridge should work in practice, and produce work worthy of publication.

THE MEUNIER HOUSE AT CALDECOTE NEAR CAMBRIDGE

"... beauty should be a novel experience, and this is rarely comfortable. This house is an attempt to achieve some sort of nobility—to create out of space, not a cosy living room, but something that elevates rather than comforts."
—John Meunier, from the Listing information on the Meunier House

As described elsewhere in this book, the University of Cambridge financially and practically supported the Meuniers in their efforts to build themselves a home. The opportunity to purchase land on an apple orchard in the countryside outside Cambridge brought with it very little of the planning constraints that influence design today. Identified as potential building land, the case did not need to be made for why a house might be constructed there, and the question of style was less vexed than today. Instead, the Meuniers faced the problem of a very limited budget. They were otherwise relatively free to project a form of situated idealism onto the land; land which offered them the possibility of building a family home, and of manifesting an architectural project grounded in ideas. As a university lecturer John was expected to produce architecture worthy of publication. Still very young, the 28 year old architect nonetheless set out to test certain of the ideas that he had absorbed as a student at Liverpool and Harvard, and to reconcile these with the culturally specific questions of building. It is my contention that it is this specificity that makes the Grade II Listed Building worthy of our contemplation still today and, I think, far superior as a piece of architecture than many of the projects produced with similar ideas at this time. In particular, what distinguishes The Meunier House from the work of Colin Rowe's students, and Peter Eisenman specifically, is its situated idealism, it's spatial contingency and it's material power. Whilst it is a deliberately conceptual project, the ideas within the design do not dominate your experience of it, and are neither literal nor too abstract. I will attempt to explain why I think that this is a remarkable artistic and theoretical achievement, one worthy of further study, and an exciting and beautiful building.

In essence, the geometric order of The Meunier House consists of two squares that overlap: a larger taller volume accommodates the "public" parts of the house; the proportionally minor square houses the more "private" three bedrooms; with the WC and bathroom situated at the point of topological congruence of the two square figures within the plan. The house is more than just the enclosed spaces though, and a larger square defines the dwelling in fundamental terms as a terracotta plinth. In fact, the idealised character of the pure "Platonic Form" of the house is reinforced by some absolutely quotidian and situational elements, grounding it in the everyday world of human affairs.

One of these, housing the bins and garden tools, is sat in the north east corner of the compound, and you pass by it, mostly unremarked as you enter. This grand shed is formed from two squares in plan, and comprised of a series

Patrick Lynch

of square tiles. The other ambiguous element within the architecture is the large brick chimney. It sits just off axis with the entrance hallway and asymmetric within the larger square volume; and yet is centred on the living room, an area that is defined furthermore by yet another change in floor surface, a rush mat (made up of square tiles of course).

Meunier initially intended to paint the bricks of his house white, until a conversation with an artist friend—Barry Gasson's first wife Liz—persuaded him otherwise[30]. Doing so would have emphasized its disconnection from the landscape, emphasizing its objecthood, and required maintenance. In contrast, the exterior blocks of the Wendon house were originally unpainted, its power deriving from the strongly tectonic presence of the vertical bays and their contrast with the striated horizontal rhythm of the mortar joints. Leaving Caldecote unpainted was one of the "best decisions" he ever made, Meunier insists, and it is hard to disagree. Furthermore, stepping the external cavity wall out over the uninsulated brick base is a master stroke of tectonic poetry. The resulting sharp horizontal line further emphasises the fall of the land across the site, and also the horizon of inhabitation established on it by the architect. This horizon is a set up at the entrance by four concrete square stepping stones, and expressed on the terrace as a bare brick plinth, creating a sense of floating above the earth, and of being thrown into the view of the landscape.

Unlike Palladio's villas, where the outbuildings are often partly buried of hidden (such as the Barchessa at the Villa Rotunda) or incorporated into elaborate colonnaded wings, you arrive by car at a brick garage, and process from there into a side entrance. The quotidian, technological and ideal aspects of a modern house are unified by the repetitive geometric figure of the squares at Caldecote, and in the persistently unchanging scale and rhythm of red flettons. The material of the house, both ground and walls, is shockingly consistent and radically modern—a sort of avant-garde vernacular, reminiscent of the buildings around Cambridge by Colin St John Wilson (and his extension to the Georgian Terrace of the architecture department at Scroope Terrace). One might (and others have, not always kindly) call this fusion of an extremely reduced material palette, uniformity and rigorous geometric form, typical of "The Cambridge School".[31]

There is, however, another dimension that I would like to emphasise here, one which transcends a stand off between physical presence and abstracted form. It is possible, I believe, to make a hermeneutic reading of the Meunier House, that sees its combination of geometry and humble materials as a linguistic nuance: evidence of a sophisticated understanding of the relationship between character and type (something that James Ackerman discusses in *The Villa: Form and Ideology of Country Houses*[32]). The house steps up in scale to emphasise the decorum and hierarchy of the living room, in imitation of a Renaissance villa, culminating in a "galleria"—a spatial type aloof from the surrounding landscape in and often complimented by a "belvedere" outside, with a "parterre" sat in between cultivated landscape, art, and architecture proper. One can make such a Hermeneutic reading of the Meunier House at Caldecote not because of anything inherently villa-like in the form of the building, or in its typology (and in fact Ackerman is insistent that villas are typified by coming in a multitude of formal types). Rather, Ackerman claims, it is the "ideology" of villas, and of their patrons and architects that distinguish these buildings. This ideology consists of reverence for a nuanced understanding of the traditions of villa life; desire for immersion in the natural world, and a degree of cultivated distance from it. A villa represents a "mentality" based on love of entertaining and an urbane rural life, stretching back to Roman society Rykwert claims[33], and is even, Vesely suggests, "a way of life".[34]

BEYOND THE FORMAL AND MATERIAL IMAGINATION

"what counts for the orientation of the spectacle is not my body as it in fact is, as a thing in objective space, but as a system of possible actions, a virtual body with its phenomenal 'place' defined by its task and situation."
—Maurice Merleau-Ponty, *Phenomenology of Perception*

I would like now to attempt to try to reveal a profound dimension of architectural culture that is characteristic of Meunier's work, one that reconciles geometry with material qualities, situating both in a philosophical tradition that recognises and celebrates the central role of spatiality and architecture in human culture.

Arguably, one of Meunier's successors at Cambridge, Dalibor Vesely, introduced what used to be called "continental philosophy" into British architectural discourse, alongside his colleague, mentor and friend Joseph Rykwert. Primarily they did this via the MA course in the History of Architecture at Essex University that Rykwert established in the 1960s and the 1970s[35]. Vesely also ran a diploma (Masters level) design studio at the Architectural Association for a decade during this period, Diploma Unit 1, and on moving to Cambridge (along with Peter Carl) he consolidated his design teaching with a complimentary series of lectures and seminars with topics ranging from Baroque Garden Design to 20th Century Surrealism. Vesely's approach was largely antithetical to formal analysis, and instead he emphasised the hermeneutic and phenomonelogical aspects of cultural experience, of which architecture is only one part.

The reputation for piety that is sometimes associated with phenomenology in architecture is perhaps largely due to the public's reception of Martin Heidegger's thinking via Norberg-Schulz. Its influence upon Kenneth Frampton, furthermore, is often characterised as a degree of "resistance" to metropolitan urbanity and to the extremes of modern technology, in favour of what Frampton (after Alexander Tzonis and Liane Lefaivre), called "critical regionalism".[36] In Frampton's work, phenomenology is sometimes elided with materiality in architecture, something that he has described, following the influence of Gottfried Semper, as "tectonic culture".[37] In each of these examples, formal analysis of building plans is to some degree complimented by, and even usurped by, close attention to the experiential qualities of architectural spatiality, even if the lexicon of 20th century architectural jargon remaining largely intact, and the antinomies of "form" and "function", "space" and "materiality" are left unchallenged, and seemingly irreconcilably distinct.

In contrast, Vesely emphasised the reciprocity of the twin phenomena of what he called "articulation" and "embodiment" (or what might be crudely compared to representation and materiality in architecture), stating that: "the silence of embodiment is always to a certain degree a voice of articulation... it is only under these conditions that we can understand the language and the cultural role of architecture".[38]

Vesely claimed that "we need to see these terms (embodiment and articulation) in their dialectical relationship", continuing:

> "The place of architecture in the continuum of culture is special because its reality coincides with the reality of primary situations and their mode of embodiment. The history of architecture can be seen as the history of attempts to represent the latent order of nature and create a plausible spatial matrix for the rest of culture. The plausibility of the spatial matrix rests on a long process of interpretations and modifications that established an identifiable tradition."[39]

He calls this place "the playing field of architecture", and suggests that "if we extend the notion of playing field to architecture, then it may be possible to say that what the playing field is to the game, architecture is to culture in its broadest sense."[40] The reason why this play is capable of reconciling what on the surface appear to be irreconcilable opposites (or "antinomies" to use Kant's phrase), can be explained by Merleau-Ponty's notion of "virtual body", Vesely argues. I am going to cite him at length, as the idea that the paradox of design creativity may be a manifestation of the paradoxical character of human experience of reality itself, as Vesely (and by inference, Merleau-Ponty) claim, overcomes false distinctions between body and world, and opens up a provocative new way to think about the reciprocity of virtual (disembodied) and physical aspects of design (and our experience of architecture and indeed reality):

"The concept of 'virtual body', defined by its tasks and situation, refers to the creative formation of space in terms not only of its topography (as a situated place), or its orientation, but also its physiognomy. Only with these aspects of architectural space in mind can we understand the deepest levels of space as it is constituted in the domain of given natural conditions and human spontaneity. On this level, spatiality is primarily dependent not on the position of the human body, but on the continuity between the actual and possible structures of the surrounding world to which the human body belongs... the horizon of all of our experiences that cannot be fully thematised in fact defines a world in which space is only a dimension. In this context it would be more appropriate to speak about the spatiality of the world so that structure, topography, orientation of space could receive their proper ontological meaning. There is no ultimate origin or ground of space, for the same reason that there is no ultimate ground of the world. Instead there is a continuum of references mediating between the more articulated and explicit forms of space and its implicit deep structure."[41]

In other words, imagination is a profound aspect of being in the world in general; and architecture has constantly, as a theory of reality and a mode of practice, sought to reveal its "deep structure".

What are the grounds for Vesely's claim that "what the playing field is to the game, architecture is to culture in its broadest sense"? Firstly, he cites the neurologist Erwin Straus[42] to demonstrate that architectural space reveals the primary character of spatiality to lie in movement:

"Sensuality and motility are coordinated in the tactile sphere in an especially striking fashion. We pass our fingers over the table-top and apprehend its smoothness as a quality of the object. The tactile impression results from the completion of the movement. When the tactile movement stops, the tactile impression dies out."[43]

Movement is not only inherent in sensuality, but also essential to embodiment generally, and this is the crucial aspect of space that enables architecture to become articulate. In spatial articulation the arts play a part in "synaesthetic experience" in the same way that all the senses are coordinated in everyday life generally. Architectural space "supports" our movement, providing stability for culture generally (as a playing field does for sportsmen):

> "We experience the most obvious manifestations of the structuring role of architecture almost constantly in our everyday lives. There is hardly a place or a circumstance that is not organised by spatial intentions (or in the case of natural surroundings, experienced as organised). The encounter with things and their spatial order is an encounter with the otherness of our situation, accessible through the dialectics of revealing and hiding.... However, we need to see these terms (embodiment and articulation) in their dialectical relationship: it is by resistance that architecture supports our intentions and the appropriate meaning of a situation. We are aware of this most intuitively each time we move up a staircase, travel through uncomfortable corridors, enter rooms with certain expectations, or recognise the purpose of a building from its layout and physiognomy."[44]

Vesely furthermore suggests that there is a play between the "silence" and "resistance" of space and the role that architecture has in "supporting" and "articulating" the "unity" of the arts in traditional buildings, which reveals the profound contribution that it has in situating and orienting us in the world. He offers some concrete architectural examples to explain the role movement plays in our experience of space and in our comprehension of the representative aspects of it (whilst noting that "the process of bringing the latent world to visibility is most clearly demonstrated in the design of gardens, where the cosmic conditions are revealed in a visible order").[45] In each, "the natural world" provides the means of and measure of experience.

Vesely links the idea of virtual body and our capacity for imaginative orientation with the ability of design to stimulate anticipation and temporal comprehension, via physical experience. He calls this phenomena "Communicative Movement", and uses the example of two architectural settings.

Firstly, the rose window on the west front at Chartres Cathedral represents the second coming of Christ (Parousia) and the fulfilment of Christian cosmogony, which began with the "incarnation of the word". Vesely insists that "the body of the cathedral provides a background for the articulation of the more explicit meanings visible in the physiognomy and iconography of the sculpture and coloured windows".[46] This articulation occurs as interplay between a relatively inarticulate rhythm of columns and arches (of the barely articulated stone architectural space), and the highly articulated rhythm established by the sun's movement (illuminating the stained glass):

> "The relationships between these levels of articulation and their equivalent
> modes of embodiment are brought together in the east to west movement
> of the sun, the visible source of light, which culminates in the sunset. The

correspondence between the Last Judgement in the rose window and the sunset illustrates very beautifully the link between the invisible phenomena of death and resurrection, their visible representation in the window, and their embodiment in the hierarchical structure of the cathedral, animated by the movement and light of the sun. The crucial observation at Chartres is how the body of the cathedral, itself abstract and silent, is capable of revealing and supporting a very subtle and highly articulated meaning of salvation—a meaning that can be brought down to earth tangibly and concretely."[47]

Vesely's other examples of "communicative movement" in architectural space involve both the description of the typical Parisian cafe as a "field of references" and as a "visible text" and a Baroque staircase.[48] The latter reveals that embodiment is movement, not simply materiality (although this plays a supporting role as "resistance" enabling and "supporting" movement).

In the case of the example of the Baroque staircase at the Bishop's Residence at Würzburg, this enigmatic complexity is a characteristic of an elaborate iconographic scheme in which the architecture of Balthasar Neumann and the frescoes of Tiepolo are unified. Both resistant stone and painted ceiling combine to situate actual and imaginary space in relationship to each other—"one art participates in the reality of the other"—and this unity is achieved through movement.[49] "The unity of space", Vesely reminds us, "depends on the continuity of references, which in our case is the continuity of embodiment understood not as the materiality of a particular art but as situatedness and participation in movement" (whose ultimate reference is "earth"). This unity "reveals the tension between the anonymity and silence of the architectural body and the iconicity that can be anticipated", and results from the "universality of the imagination" that enables architect and artist to anticipate the culmination of each other's efforts, which in this case occurs on the landing of the staircase at which point it becomes clear that the ceiling represents an image that resolves itself through "communicative movement":

"What we can understand through our experience is the structure of the articulated world in which we can directly participate. This is precisely what we do when we move through the foyer and enter the ceremonial stair hall. The staircase itself is aligned with the movement of the sun, represented by Apollo; this gives orientation not only to the staircase but to the room as a whole. As we ascend to the first landing and turn, the staircase becomes part of the structure of the room; the four walls transform themselves into four continents and eventually disappear into the light of the ceiling."[50]

However, embodiment is body-in-movement and since "situation is communication", our bodily situations provide a clue to the nature of decorum.

Vesely alludes to this as the role that "decor" plays in architecture, and it is significant that in the architectural examples he offers of "communicative space", artworks play a vital role in revealing the "reciprocity between the

This page:
The Bishop's Residence at Würzburg, Treppenhaus, with fresco by Tiepolo,
Apollo and his Continents, 1752–1753.   The Horizon of the Long Now   249

articulated world and its embodiment". He suggests that this reveals "Heidegger's effort to grasp" the significance of "earth" and the role that "the work of art" plays in situating World and Being in relation to each other:

> "The setting up a world, does not cause the material to disappear, but rather causes it to come forth for the very first time and to come open of the work's world. The rock comes to bear and rest and so first becomes rock; metals come to glitter and shimmer, colours to glow, tones to sing, the word to speak. All this comes forth as the work sets itself back into massiveness and heaviness of stone, into the firmness and pliancy of wood, into the luster of metal, into the lighting and darkening of colour, into the clang of tone, and into the naming of the word".[51]

Vesely also situates geometry and "resonance" as aspects of spatiality that place architecture as central to the formation of communicative culture generally. Both aspects of communicative space are closely related to rhythm and to proportion, he suggests.[52] He contends that "what logic and grammar are to verbal language, geometry is to the visual world", asserting the central role that it played in pre-Enlightenment culture "on the boundary of visible realities".[53] Vesely suggests that "geometry is subtly linked to language by movement and gesture" and that "even at its most abstract level, geometry depends on certain basic movements and gestures, such as measuring and drawing, visual analysis, and making models".[54]

Architecture exhibits aspects of "communicative movement" in a number of ways; not only as spatial experience in a finished building, but in the corporeal and imaginative act of design, which can be seen as a form of orientation in the world in itself. Like craft or sport, design is a mode of "communicative movement". Resonance and rhythm are aspects also of relationships that imply orientation as decorum, and as such are seen by Vesely as part of a hierarchy of relationships implied by the analogical imagination, representing "the communicative nature of movement, imagination, and language".[55]

"Someone asked me if the Meunier house is 'cosy'? I replied:
'No, but the spaces make me feel good (a feeling of harmony)'."[56]
—Hans Munthe-Kaas, Mathematician (and current resident
of the Meunier House)

I hope to have shown that the somewhat hokey opposition of The Formal vs. Material imagination obscures architecture's full potential to deepen one's experience of the world, and understanding of being human. What is revealed instead I suggest, is a situated appreciation of the world—contemplation even— of the shared conditions of humanity; reflection upon a common horizon of human finitude.

In relation to Meunier's architecture, the quality of what he calls "building worthy of contemplation" (see "Foothold" above) occurs in a number of places in particular, I believe. As noted by Meunier, firstly this emerged in the relationships that are revealed between the Caldecote House, the orchard, and the next door and neighbouring churches. One's experience of the landscape of human time is heightened: husbandry, myth and material culture are situated on a common horizon. The house is itself almost all horizon. One's distance from, and place within, an English medieval village is laid bare: viewed from the terrace threshold of the house, inhabitants are protected in part from, but ultimately exposed to, a world of recurrence and deterioration, renewal and decay.

The Burrell Collection (to paraphrase some observations above) seems to me to unite the themes of climate as well as topography; the role of the sun's energy as an essential form of rhythm in architecture—not to mention the rhythms of everyday life, custom, habit, civic culture as festival, etc.—with another dimension of time: history. The building situates fragments from the history of architecture in relation to antique artefacts, placing a chronological narrative in tension with Pollok Country Park, both its historic and natural setting. In the audacious modesty of simply reusing things on the one hand (the

archaic power of the entrance gable that you come across like a fragment of a dream); and then the frank confrontation of ancient objects and the verdant forest the project reveals the analogical character of memory and imagination, and says as much about how we see the world as any cubist painting or philosophy of time. This experience is an intentional spatial narrative I believe, designed to make one recognise and witness something specific: an existential, phenomenological architecture made up of moments, thresholds, pauses, changes of atmosphere, both physical and psychic.

At the Gordon House, built into and springing from a mountain in Cincinnati, the piano nobile both exposes and protects its urbane inhabitant. Its Intricate armature establishes her within a territory of civic architectural decorum, precisely poised as part of the deep horizon of the city.

At the Meuniers' home in Arizona, the luscious garden and shady terraces open onto a view of a not too far distant mountain, offering stark evidence of a much older scale of time, something much older than a medieval village; something pre-human, pre-historical, pre-modern.

In each case, the situated, ontological character of architecture is at its most potent. We are situated somewhere in between the past and the future, somewhere more interesting and beautiful, I believe, than discussions about form or matter, modernism or postmodernism, situated within a horizon "of the universal and the particular"[57]; witnesses to the Intricate, embodied, silent articulation of what is sometimes called "the long now".[58]

I would like to reiterate and to conclude with one of John Meunier's very generous, Intricate and modest responses to my observations about his work, something which I think summarises and demonstrates his profound achievements as a designer, teacher and thinker: "Two things are raised here: the notion of connection to the larger world both in space and in time; and the notion of structured sensory and intellectual experience as the goal of architecture. They are both very important to me."[59]

Chronology

Work

1963
Meunier House
Caldecote, UK

1964
Wendon House
Cambridge, UK

1964
Edington House
Cambridge, UK

1964
Sports Pavilion
University of Essex
Essex, UK

1964
Housing project
Heacham, UK

1974
New Hall College
Cambridge, UK

1974
Burrell Museum
Glasgow, UK

1984
Gordon House on Mount Adam
Cincinnati, USA

2010
Solana Beach
California, USA

Life

NOTTINGHAM, SOUTHPORT, AND LIVERPOOL

1936
Born on June 17th in Nottingham, moved to Southport in 1939 at the outbreak of WWII.

1947-1953
King George Vth Grammar School, Southport, in the *Transitus* fast-track.

1953-1957
Liverpool University School of Architecture; played tennis, briefly, for the University.

NEW YORK

1957-1958
Worked for Marcel Breuer in New York mostly on St. John's Abbey in Wisconsin, and met Dorothy Donnelly recent Graduate of Barnard College, Columbia University, who also played tennis. Also worked evenings and weekends with Peter Blake and Julian Neski on their design for the Toronto City Hall Competition, and for Paul Lester Weiner of Town Planning Associates on their housing project near Washington Square, Manhattan.

1958
Three-month solo tour of the United States and Canada on a second-hand Vespa Motor Scooter.

LIVERPOOL AND LONDON

1958-1959
Completed studies at Liverpool University School of Architecture and graduated with a First Class Honours degree.

1959
Worked in the Ministry of Education Development Group, Curzon Street, London.

HARVARD

1959-1960
Frank Knox Fellowship to Harvard Graduate School of Design. Graduated MArch.

1960
Married Dorothy Donnelly in New York on February 6th during semester break.

| 1960 | Worked with Serge Chermayeff and Christopher Alexander on *Community and Privacy* in the Joint Institute for Urban Studies of Harvard and MIT. |

MUNICH

| 1960-1962 | Worked in the office of Fred Angerer, mostly on the design of the Bayerische Gemeindebank. He was a Professor of *Kleine Stadtebau und Industrie Bau* at the Technical University in Munich. |
| 1962 | Registered Architect Land Bayern, West Germany. |

CAMBRIDGE

1962	Appointed to an Assistant Lectureship in the School of Architecture at Cambridge University and awarded the degree of MA as required for appointment to the faculty.
1963-1965	Designed and built as the general contractor our house in the hamlet of Caldecote, 7.5 miles from the School, with the assistance from Cambridge University of a second mortgage up to 100% of the value of the house and land. The house was initially published in *The Architectural Review*, *House and Garden*, and *The Observer Magazine*, all in 1968. It is now a Grade II Listed Building.
1964	Associate Royal Institute of British Architects, ARCUK # 000 32297k.
1964-1966	In partnership with Barry Gasson designed the Wendon House in the village of Barton near Cambridge. The house was published in *The Architects Journal*, *House and Garden*, *Bauen und Wohnen* and was selected by the British Council to be exhibited at the Paris Biennale in 1967. It too is a Grade II Listed Building.
1964-1974	In partnership with Barry Gasson designed several buildings and projects, including the Edington House in Little Eversden, published in *The Architectural Review* and *House and Garden*; a Sports Pavilion for the University of Essex, published in *The Architectural Review*; a Master Plan and student accommodation re-design for Trinity Hall college, Cambridge; and a housing project on land in the village of Heacham

owned by Gonville and Caius College, Cambridge. Our partnership culminated after winning the competition and the commission for the Burrell Museum in Glasgow, initially published in 1972 by *The Architect's Journal*, *The RIBA Journal*, *Design*, *Architectural Design*, and the *Museums Journal*. After the building was completed in 1984 it was widely published in journals such as *The Architectural Review* and *Country Life*.

1966 Granted a tenured faculty position until June 2001 as Lecturer in Architecture at Cambridge University.

1967-1976 Elected a Fellow and Member of the Council of Darwin College, Cambridge, where I later became Chairman of the Research Fellowship Selection Committee.

1968-1969 Sabbatical leave in the Autumn and Spring Terms during which I was an invited visiting faculty member at the Graduate School of Design of Harvard University, The School of Architecture at Yale University, and California State Polytechnic in San Luis Obispo.

1969 Councilor Caldecote Parish Council and Chairman of Caldecote Primary School PTA.

1969-1972 Secretary of the Faculty Board of Fine Arts (later called the Faculty of Architecture and History of Western Art) and its Degree Committee and Member and Secretary of the Appointments Committee.

1970 Meunier and Wendon Houses in *Cambridge New Architecture* published by Leonard Hill, London.

1971-1976 Board of Architectural Education and Practice and Honorary officer of the Steering Committee and The Monopolies Commission Steering Group. Appointed to RIBA Visiting Boards at: Architectural Association, North East London Polytechnic, Northern Polytechnic, Hull School of Architecture, Cheltenham School of Architecture, Edinburgh University.

1974-76 Member of FORUM (group of 50 leading British Architects) Association of Consultant Architects.

1974-5 Appointed Interim Head of the Department of Architecture at Cambridge University following the accidental death of Professor Bill Howell.

1974 -1976	In partnership with David Handlin designed a revised Master Plan and Student Housing for what was then New Hall College, Cambridge. Published in *The Architect's Journal*.

CINCINNATI

1976	Having been previously interviewed for administrative positions at Cornell University and MIT accepted the Chair of Architecture, later the Directorship of the School of Architecture and Interior Design, in the College of Design, Architecture, Art and Planning at the University of Cincinnati in the United States. The university is well-known for its innovative co-op program in many professional fields alternating three months in paid internships in major national and international firms with three months in academia. A version of the "thick-sandwich" courses I had grown to respect on my earlier accreditation visits to Polytechnic Schools of Architecture in the UK.
1976-1979	Member of the University Research Council, at the University of Cincinnati.
1979-1980	Chairman of the Guidelines Subcommittee of the Urban Conservation Task Force, City of Cincinnati and Member of the Mayor's Economic Development Task Force.
1980-1987	Visiting Critic at the Universities of Harvard, McGill, Virginia, Kentucky, Miami, Ohio State; and Distinguished Visiting Lecturer in Architectural History at the University of North Carolina at Charlotte.
1980 -82	Chairman of the Academic Workshops at the Association of the Collegiate Schools of Architecture (ACSA) Annual Meetings in San Antonio Texas and in Quebec, Ontario, Canada, also Member of the ACSA Publications Committee.
1980–1989	National Architectural Accrediting Board member on Visiting Teams to: Illinois Institute of Technology, Pratt Institute, SCI-Arc, Drury College, California Polytechnic University SLO, Hampton Institute, SUNY Buffalo, Cooper Union, Iowa State.
1980	Executive Editor *CENTRAL Papers on Architecture*.
1981	Master Plan for the College of Design, Architecture, Art, and Planning at the University of Cincinnati, the basis for the design of a major extension by Peter Eisenman.

1981	After nomination by Professor Peter Collins of McGill elected as a Fellow of the Royal Society of Arts in London, UK. I had got to know Professor Collins during visits to McGill where I taught "In the Manner Of" design studios for several years. Peter Collins was also one of several distinguished visiting faculty such as Colin Rowe, Frank Duffy and Stanley Tigerman we invited for extended stays in Cincinnati.
1982	Infill housing study for the Walnut Hills Redevelopment Foundation on Sinton Avenue and Nassau Street in Cincinnati, Ohio.
1982-1984	Design of the Gordon House on Mount Adams overlooking downtown Cincinnati.
1983-1987	Member of the Academic Affairs Committee and the Planning Committee of the Faculty Senate of the University of Cincinnati.
1984	Feasibility Study and Preliminary Design for the Prints, Drawings, and Photographic Collection of the Cincinnati Art Museum.
1985-1987	President of The Miami Purchase Association for Historic Preservation.
1985-1987	Advisor to the Cincinnati City Planning Commission, Member of the Urban Design Review Board, Cincinnati Bicentennial Commission, Cincinnati Preservation Awards Committee, Advisory Committee to the Hillsides Trust.
1987 -1992	Beginning with a meeting in Cranbrook, Michigan, which I wrote up for the *Journal of Architectural Education* (JAE), there was more and more involvement with The Association of Collegiate Schools of Architecture (all the accredited architecture schools in both the USA and Canada) culminating in a three year stint as President Elect, President, (1991-1992), and Past President.

PHOENIX ARIZONA

1987-2002	Dean of the College of Architecture and Environmental Design at Arizona State University including Architecture, Planning, Industrial Design, and Interior Design. During my tenure Landscape Architecture, Graphic Design, and Environmental Resource Management were added. All the professional programs were nationally accredited and ranked.

1987-2002	Chair of the Design Review Board, later the Public Art and Design Review Council, of Arizona State University with responsibilities in architect/artist selection as well as design review.
1987-1990	Member Downtown Planning and Transportation Sub-committee of the City of Phoenix.
1989	Established, with the approval of the Board of Regents of all the Arizona Universities, the Herberger Center for Design Excellence, the research and publication arm of the College of Architecture and Environmental Design, with an initial endowment of $500,000, and an annual budget from the Provost's Office of $135,000. Also The Council for Design Excellence, a support group from community leaders each contributing annually $1,000.
1989	Established the Joint Urban Design Program, with studios at the ASU Downtown Center and in the College, with contracts for studies with the cities of Phoenix, Scottsdale, Peoria, Tempe, and the Motorola Corporation.
1989-2002	Vice-Chair of the Central City Board of Architectural Review appointed by the City Manager of Phoenix, with responsibilities in architect selection for buildings such as the city library, the art museum, the science museum, the history museum, the Phoenix theatre.
1989-1990	Member of the Policy Committee and Chair of the Urban Task Force of the Phoenix Futures Forum assembled by the Mayor of the city of Phoenix.
1989-2002	Board Member of the Phoenix Community Alliance.
1993-1995	Approval from the Board of Regents for an Interdisciplinary PhD program in the College established with an initial endowment from the Herberger family of $500,000.
1993	Invited by the Vice-President for Student Affairs to plan the University's first academic residential college, associated with the College of Architecture and Environmental Design. It was eventually called the Athena Program.
1993-1994	Anchor/commentator of a six-part series on the Horizon program of KAET Public Television, "The APS Environmental Showcase Home".
1993	A series of commentaries on the KAET Horizon program, including "Frank Lloyd Wright's Arizona Legacy"

1993	Registered Architect #27526 State of Arizona, NCARB Certificate #43,867.
1994	Member of the American Institute of Architects (AIA).
1994-1997	Board Member of the National Architectural Accrediting Board (NAAB).
1995-2006	Appointed as a Peer Professional within the Federal GSA Design Excellence Program selecting architects and conducting design review of Federal Courthouse Projects in: Phoenix, Tucson, Albuquerque, Laredo, Salt Lake City, Corpus Christi, El Paso.
1995	Together with Professor Michael Underhill designed a study for a new building for the College of Public Programs.
1995-1997	Together with Professor Ron McCoy and Janet Simon designed a study for the redesign of Sun Devil football stadium which at that time was the home not only of the Arizona State University football team but also the National Football League team, the Arizona Cardinals. When the latter team found the support for a new stadium my advice was sought and Peter Eisenman was appointed as the Design Architect. He and I had been colleagues at Cambridge, but he was also a great fan of football and was selected from my list by the owners of the team.
1998	Again together with Professor Ron McCoy and Janet Simon we prepared a Master Plan for the development of University property along the river front of the Rio Salado.
1998-2001	Initiated the Desert Cities Dinners, with speakers Joel Garreau, Paul Goldberger, and Moshe Safdie to raise funds to support the College. Travelled to Israel to film and interview Moshe Safdie for an introduction to his presentation.
2001-2002	At the end of my 15year term as Dean of the College of Architecture and Environmental Design I took a year's Sabbatical Leave and travelled widely in Iran, India, Egypt, Tunisia, Morocco, Yemen, Australia, Chile and Peru researching Desert Cities. I was studying historic Desert Cities, but also filming them. The Chapter on *Making Desert Cities* that appears earlier in this book was a product, but also there were several videos that have been widely marketed by Insight Media, mostly to academia. An episode of the History Channel on American television was devoted to this work.

2002-2017	Professor of Architecture, The School of Design, Herberger Institute for Design and the Arts, Arizona State University, with special responsibilities within the 3+ Program, our fast-track professional MArch degree program for mature students with undergraduate degrees in other disciplines.
2010	Designed a new home for our son, (an orthopaedic surgeon and clinical professor at the University of California in San Diego) and his family in Solana Beach, California.

SOUTH CAROLINA

2005-2006	Visiting Director of the School of Architecture at Clemson University.

CAMBRIDGE

2004	Designed and built a major extension and new wing to the house in Caldecote making it possible to accommodate visiting family and friends in the original bedroom wing.
2008-2009	Sabbatical leave pursuing research on Intricacy, using the libraries of Cambridge University with visits to Paris, Edinburgh, Stowe, Utrecht etc. to make in-depth case studies. This research generated a series of seminars and a book proposal to Routledge. It now informs a major theme of this book.

SEMESTER AT SEA

2014	Professor of Architecture and Urbanism on a three-month voyage starting in Southampton and ending in Fort Lauderdale, Florida, visiting St. Petersburg, Gdansk, Rostock, Antwerp, Le Havre, Dublin, Lisbon, Cadiz, Casablanca, Rome, Venice, Barcelona, Rio de Janeiro, Bridgetown, and Havana. My courses were accredited by the University of Virginia who had the franchise for this voyage, making it possible for the students from many different universities to transfer credit.

2017 -   Emeritus Professor of Architecture at Arizona State University with homes both in Arizona and the UK. Attempting to defend the Burrell Museum from negative alterations and amendments during its current restoration and redesign has been a time consuming, if frustrating, task, but it has introduced me to the editor and co-author of this book and of his Journal of Civic Architecture which has also published some of my work.

List of Publications

Design Project Reviews

"Three Ways to Plan for Progressive Patient Care," *The Modern Hospital*, Vol. 95, No. 6, December 1960, pp. 82–85

"In a Cambridgeshire Orchard," *The Architectural Review*, Vol. 144, No. 858, August, 1968, pp. 106–107

"Wohnhaus in Boston/Cambridgeshire, England," *Bauen & Wohnen*. 24. Jahrgang, December, 1970, Heft 12. pp. 440–441

"University of Essex Sports Pavilion," *The Architectural Review*, Vol. 147, No. 878, April 1970, p. 270

"An Architect's own house near Cambridge," *House and Garden*, Vol. 23, April 1968, pp. 98–101

"A House is more than a set of rooms," *The Observer Magazine*, London, 12 May 1968, pp. 26, 29

"Burrell Collection Competition," *The Architect's Journal*, No. 12, Vol. 155, 22 March 1972, pp. 590-595; *RIBA Journal*, August 1972, pp. 327-329; *Design*, May 1972, p. 26; *Architectural Design*, April 1972, p. 256; *Museum's Journal*, December 1972, pp. 104–106

"The Burrell: Art and Nature," Jonathan Glancey, *The Architectural Review*, Vol. 175, No. 1044, February 1984, pp. 28–37

"Doing the Old Man Proud—the Burrell Collection, Glasgow," *Country Life*, January, 1984

"A Long Low House Set in an Apple Orchard," *House and Garden*, November 1974, pp. 112-115

"House at Little Eversden, Cambridgeshire," *The Architectural Review,* April 1974, pp. 232-234

"Cambridge Style," *The Architect's Journal*, September, 1979, pp. 586-587

"Meunier House", "Wendon House", *Cambridge New Architecture*, Philip Booth and Nicholas Taylor, Leonard Hill, London, 1970, pp. 196–198, 199–200

Texts by John Meunier

"Architecture," ed. Klaus Boehm, *University Choice*, Penguin, 1966, pp. 39–49.

"Ten new areas of architectural thought," *Architecture: Opportunities, Achievements*, RIBA Publications, 1977, pp. 22–23

"The Cranbrook TS: Notes from Albion," *Journal of Architectural Education*, Vol. 31, No. 3, pp. 16–17

"Master classes with Charles Moore, et al," *RIBA Journal*, February 1978, pp, 67-68

"The Cranbrook TS: Old Albion Strikes Again," *Journal of Architectural Education*, Vol. 32, No. 3, pp. 12, 13, 33, 34

Review of P.L. Nervi's "Aesthetics and Technology in Building," for *Italian Studies*, Vol. 23, Oxford University Press, 1968

Review of Norberg-Schulz's "Existence Space and Architecture," *RIBA Journal*, October 1971

"Teaching Design and Technology in the First Two Years," *Journal of Architectural Education*, Vol. 34, No. 2, Winter 1980

With Bertram Berenson, "House on the Hill," *The Cincinnati Enquirer*, 28 January, 1984

"'In the Manner of' À Propos de 'À la Façon de'," *The Fifth Column, The Canadian Student Journal of Architecture*, Vol. 4, No. 1, Automne 1983

"Paradigms for Practice: A Task for Architecture Schools," *Jubilee Issue Journal of Architectural Education*, Vol. 40, No. 2, ed. David Bell, 1987

Review of Peter G. Rowe's "Design Thinking," *Triglyph—a Southwestern Journal of Architecture and Environmental Design*, No. 6, ed. Marcus Whiffen, Summer 1988

Introduction to *The City of the 21st Century*, ed. Madis Pihlak, proceedings of a conference held at Arizona State University, April 1988

"Thoughts on Preparations for Tenure for Design Faculty," *Debate and Dialogue: Architectural Design and Pedagogy. Proceedings of the 77th Annual Meeting of the ACSA*, 1989

"A Matter of Time: The Relationship between Architecture and Interior Design," *Designers West*, Vol. 38, No. 2, December 1990

"Phoenix's Two Ecologies", *Arizona Business and Development*, July 1991

"Autos Spawned the New Urban Age," review of *Edge City, Life on the New Frontier* by Joel Garreau, *Arizona Business Gazette*, November 1991

"Downtown Stadium offers Huge Potential," op ed piece in *The Arizona Republic*, December 1993

"Lost Phoenix," commentary on *Horizon*, KAET public Television, 1993

"Frank Lloyd Wright's Arizona Legacy," commentary on *Horizon*, KAET public television, 1993

"The APS Environmental Showcase Home," anchor commentator, six episodes on *Horizon*, KAET public television, 1993

Introduction, *ASU's College of Architecture: The First 25 Years*, James Elmore, Herberger Center, ASU, 1994

"University Based Design Clinics as a National Resource: Measurement," *Vitalizing University-based Community Design Clinics by Organizing Them as a National Resource*, Special Focus Session ACSA Annual Meeting, March 1994

"Public and Private: Making a Better City", *Urban Design: Reshaping our Cities*, ed. Anne Vernez-Moudon and Wayne Attoe, University of Washington, 1995

"Reflections on Architecture as a Knowledge Based Discipline", *PRACTICES 3/4*, Center for the Study of the Practice of Architecture, University of Cincinnati, 1995

Introduction and chapter in *Frank Lloyd Wright: The Phoenix Papers*, Herberger Center, ASU, University of Arizona Press, 1995

Foreword, *The Environment Comes Home: Arizona Public Service's Environmental Showcase Home*, ed. David Pijawka and Kim Shetter, Herberger Center, ASU, University of Arizona Press, 1995

"Four Rules Used in the Selection of Architects", *Business Journal*, Arizona, July 1995

Introduction, *Wright in Arizona: The Early Work of Pedro E. Guerrero*, Herberger Center, ASU, 1996

Introduction, *Phoenix in Perspective: Reflections on Developing the Desert*, Grady Gammage Jr., Herberger Center, ASU, 1999

Introduction, *Desert Cities: Water, Politics and Design*, Paul Goldberger, Herberger Center, ASU, 1999

Anchor Commentator *Desert Cities 3: Phoenix/Jerusalem*, KAET Public Television, 2000

"Making Desert Cities", ed. Paul Lusk and Alf Simon, *Building To Endure: Design Lessons of Arid Lands*, University of New Mexico Press, 2009; ed. David Pijawka and Martin Gromulat, *Understanding Sustainable Cities: Concepts, Cases, and Solutions*, Kendall Hunt, 2012; ed. Christina Noble, *AzF5 Arizona Forum*, AIA Arizona, 2015

Notes

The Long Game

1   Gadamer, Hans-Georg, *Truth and Method*, London: Sheed and Ward, 1993 (1960), p.116.

2   "Anth - is a prefix derived from the Ancient Greek ἄνθος (anthos) meaning 'flower'": https://en.wikipedia.org/wiki/Antho- (accessed 8th July 2019, 14.34).

3   Cf., 'This is what the Greeks called *theoria*: to have been given away to something that in virtue of its overwhelming presence is accessible to all in common and that is distinguished in such a way that in contrast to all other goods it is not diminished by being shared and so is not an object of dispute like all other goods but actually gains through participation. In the end, this is the birth of the concept of reason: the more what is desirable is displayed for all in a way that is convincing to all, the more those involved discover themselves in this common reality: to that extent human beings possess freedom in the positive sense, they have their true identity in that common reality.', Gadamer, Hans-Georg, "What is Practice? The Conditions of Social Reason", *Reason in the Age of Science*, Cambridge, MA: MIT Press, 2001, p 77.

4   Gadamer, *Truth and Method*, Op. Cit., p.490.

On Intricacy

1   "A bicycle shed is a building; Lincoln Cathedral is a piece of architecture. Nearly everything that encloses space on a scale sufficient for a human being to move in is a building; the term architecture applies only to buildings designed with a view to aesthetic appeal.", *An Outline of European Architecture*, Nikolaus Pevsner, 1943,p.1.

2   See *Intricacy: A Project By Greg Lynn*, University of Pennsylvania Institute of Contemporary Art, 2003.

3   See *Complexity and Contradiction in Architecture*, Robert Venturi, The Museum of Modern Art, New York, 1966.

4   See *On the Art of Building in Ten Books*, Leon Battista Alberti, translated by Joseph Rykwert, Neil Leach, Robert Tavernor, MIT, 1988; and *On Alberti and the Art of Building*, Robert Tavernor, Yale, 1998.

5   See for example *The Visible and the Invisible*, Maurice Merleau-Ponty, North Western University Press, 1968 and *Body, Community, Language, World*, Jan Patoka, Chicago, 1998.

6   *The Scottish Parliament*, Charles Jencks, Scala Publishers, 2005, p.13.

7   *The True Principles of Pointed or Christian Architecture and An Apology for The Revival of Christian*

Architecture, A.W. Pugin and Roderick O'Donnell, Gracewing Publishing, 2003; *The Seven Lamps of Architecture*, John Ruskin, Penguin, 2017, etc.

8   In relatively recent times we have, of course, had the High-Tech movement, whereby architects such as Richard Rogers and Renzo Piano (and the engineer Peter Rice), have developed an aesthetic derived from the rich interplay of the constructional systems that support, enclose, and service buildings. Much of the aesthetic of early modernism for example valued simple white geometric form so that, for example, when Le Corbusier's Villa Savoie was left in great disrepair after the Second World War we discovered to our dismay that it had been built of stuccoed masonry blocks on a rough concrete frame. Second is that much of construction that is not intended to be revealed is an inherently messy process, with relatively large dimensional tolerances and little visual order, and that this reduces its production cost. Once the decision is made to reveal construction and to make it a part of the aesthetic of the building then its cost goes up as the desirable quality of finish and the desire to bring some visual order to the relationships between the components require greater time, care, and material cost.

9   Cf. "The metaphor with which I have been concerned with is more extended—a double one—in that it involves three terms, a body is like a building and the building in turn is like the world.", *The Dancing Column: On Order in Architecture*, Joseph Rykwert, MIT, 1998.

10 Cf. *The Eyes of the Skin: Architecture and the Senses*, Juhani Pallasma, John Wiley and Sons, London, 2012.

11 See the chapter "Communicative Space" in *Architecture in the Age of Divided Representation: The Question of Creativity in the Shadow of Production*, Dalibor MIT Press, 2004.

12 Cf. *The Relevance of the Beautiful and Other Essays*, Hans-Georg Gadamer, Cambridge University Press, 1988; and the chapter "Play as the Clue to Ontological Explanation" in *Truth and Method*, Shead and Ward, Hans-Georg Gadamer, London, 1960; as well as the chapter "The City Gives a Definite Direction to Nature: Decorum, Temporality and Urbanity" in *Civic Ground: Rhythmic Spatiality and the Communicative Movement Between Architecture, Sculpture and Site*, Patrick Lynch, Artifice Books on Architecture, London, 2017.

13 It is generally accepted that Stirling owed a debt to Konstantin Melnikov, whose design for the Rusakov Club (1927-29) revealed in a similar way the canted floors of the auditoria at the top of the building. Much of the work of the Russian Constructivists, such as the design for the Leningrad Pravda Building (1924) by the Vesnin brothers was similarly revelatory and sought to articulate a cultural dimension of Communist modernity.

14 See *Town Hall, Saynatsalo: Alvar Aalto* (Architecture in Detail), Richard Weston, Phaidon, 1993.

Making Desert Cities

1   *House Form and Culture*, Amos Rapaport, Prentice Hall, Englewood Cliffs, N.J., 1969. *Arabic-Islamic Cities: Building and Planning Principles,* Besim Selim Hakim, London and New York, KPI, 1986

2   *Greater Phoenix Regional Atlas: A Preview of the Region's 50-year Future*, Greater Phoenix 2100, Morrison Institue for Public Policy, ASU, Tempe, AZ, 2003

3   *Building Jaipur: The Making of an Indian City*, Vibhuti Sachdev and Giles Tillotson, Reaktion, London, 2002

4   *6,000 years of Housing*, Norbert Schoenauer, Garland STPM Press, New York, 1981

5   *La Ciudad Chilena del Siglo XVII Buenos Aires*, Gabriel Guarda, Centro Editor de America Latina, 1968

6   *Cities and Planning in the Ancient Near East*, Paul Lampl, Braziller, New York, 1968. Hakim, *Arabic-Islamic Cities: Building and Planning Principles.*

7   *Living with the Desert: Working Building of the Iranian Plateau*, Elisabeth Beasley and Michael Harverson with Susan Roaf, Aris and Phillips, Warminster, Wilts, England, 1982

8   *Sana'a: An Arabian Islamic City*, ed. R.B. Serjeant and Ronald Lewcock, World of Islam Festival Trust, London, 1983

9   *Wadi Hadramawt and the Walled City of Shibam* Paris, Ronald Lewcock, UNESCO, 1986

10 *History, Art and Architecture of Jaisalmer*, R.A. Agarawala, Agam Kala Prakashan, Delhi, 1979. Sachdev and Tillotson, *Building Jaipur: The Making of an Indian City*.

11 Guarda, *La Ciudad Chilena del Siglo XVII Buenos Aires*

The Intricate Work of Architecture

1   Gadamer, *Truth and Method*, Op. Cit., p.13.

2   I have written about this problematic phenomena at length, and its disastrous effects on the quality of our cities, in *Civic Ground: Rhythmic Spatiality and the Communicative Movement between Architecture, Sculpture and Site*, Lynch, P, Artifice Books on Architecture, London, 2017.

3   Gadamer, *Truth and Method*, Op. Cit., pp.124–5.

4   See Lynch, *Civic Ground*, Op. Cit., pp.12–13.

5   Cf., "the prior knowledge involved in a techne cannot be called 'theoretical', especially since experience is automatically acquired in using this knowledge. For, as knowledge, it is always related to practical application, and even if recalcitrant material does not always obey the person who has learnt his craft, Aristotle can still rightly quote the words of the poet: 'Techne love tyche (luck) and Tyche loves techne.' This means that the person who has been taught.', Gadamer, *Truth and Method*, Op. Cit., p 315.

6   Ibid., pp. 13–14.

Intricacy and Collaboration in my Work with Others

1   See "Intricacy and Collaboration at the Schroeder House".

2   It was my colleague Barry Gasson's first wife, Liz Gasson, a talented American painter and close friend of ours, who suggested to me that contrary to my initial intention to paint them white, we should leave the bricks at Caldecote unpainted as their multi-colours contained the palette of the other materials in the house; an inspired and amicable intervention, and another example of the value of Intricate relationships in intensifying the Intricacy and coherence of a design.

3   Initially the competition winning project was presented as a collaboration. See for example the RIBA Library Index which lists these publication. Barry Gasson and John Meunier: "Burrell Collection Competition" *The Architect's Journal*, No. 12, Vol. 155, 22 March 1972, pp. 590- 595; *RIBA Journal*, August 1972, pp. 327-329; *Design*, May 1972, p. 26; *Architectural Design*, April 1972, p. 256; *Museum's Journal*, December 1972, pp. 104-106. However, the completed building was published under the sole authorship of Barry Gasson in "The Burrell: Art and Nature", Jonathan Glancey, *The Architectural Review*, Vol. CLXXV, No. 1044, February 1984

The Horizon of the Long Now

1   For a broad and very interesting discussion of the topic of different type of imagination see *Poetics of Imagining: From Modern to Postmodern*, Richard Kearney, (1991), Edinburgh University Press, 1998.

2   See "The Wobble: The Cat with Nine Lives": in discussion with Peter Eisenman, Mark Wigley claimed that Dalibor Vesely had assaulted Eisenmans" "alma mater", and that "Rykwert is an antiquarian"—at a graduate seminar at Columbia University School Architecture, September 2012.

3   Email from John Meunier to Patrick Lynch, 28th October 2019.

4   See "Foothold" above, and in issue 2 of *The Journal of Civic Architecture*, Canalside Press, London, 2018,.

5   *Architecture in the Age of Divided Representation: The Question of Creativity in the Shadow of Production*, Dalibor Vesely, MIT Press, 2004, pp 91–92.

6   *Architectural Principles in the Age of Humanism*, Rudolf Wittkower, (1949), Academy Editions, 1998.

7   See *The Civilization of the Renaissance in Italy*, Jacob Burkhardt, Penguin, 1990; *Renaissance and Baroque*,

Heinrich Wölfflin, Collins, 1984; *Perspective as Symbolic Form*, Erwin Panofsky, Zone Books, 1997, etc.

8   See for example, *The Formal Basis of Modern Architecture*, Eisenman, Peter, PhD Dissertation, Cambridge University, 1963; Facsimile published by Lars Muller, 2006, p.29.

9   See *Alberti and the Art of Building*, Robert Tavernor, Yale, 1998.

10   *On the Art of Building in Ten Books*, Leon Battista Alberti, translated by Joseph Rykwert, Neil Leach, Robert Tavernor, MIT, 1988 *Book Nine: Ornament to Private Buildings* (411, 162-175v), pp. 298-319.

11   See "The Second Book", *The Four Books on Architecture*, Andrea Palladio, (1570), translated by Robert Tavenor and Richard Schofield, MIT, 1997.

12   See *Palladio and Palladianism*, Robert Tavernor, Thames and Hudos, 1991.

13   See "The Sacrifice of Space", David Leatherbarrow, and "Praxis: Horizons of Involvement", Peter Carl, both in *Common Ground: A Critical Reader*, ed. David Chipperfield, Kieran Long and Shumi Bose, 13th International Architecture Exhibition, La Biennale di Venezia: Marsilio, 2012; and *Architecture Oriented Otherwise*, David Leatherbarrow, Princeton University Press, 2009; *In Search of Florentine Civic Humanism: Essays on the Transition from Medieval to Modern Thought*, vol I, Hans Baron, Princeton University Press, 1980; *The*

Understanding of Ornament in the Italian Renaissance, Clare Lapraik Guest, Brill: The Netherlands, 2015; see also *The Ethical Function of Architecture*, Karsten Harries, MIT Press, 1998; "Civic Architecture", Patrick Lynch, in *Mimesis*, ed. Patrick Lynch, Artifice Books on Architecture, London, 2015; *Renovatio Urbis: Architecture, Urbanism and Ceremony in the Rome of Julius II*, Nick Temple, Routledge, 2011.

14   See for example "The methodological approaches of Colin Rowe: the multifaceted, intellectual connoisseur at La Tourette", Raúl Martínez Martínez, *arq*, vol 22, no 3, 2018, for a discussion of the various influences upon Rowe's thought.

15   "Colin Rowe, Peter Foggo, Jim Stirling, and his good friend Robert Maxwell (also a good friend of mine and the Dean at Princeton) were all students at Liverpool, not just teachers. The distinction is important because it means that the strength of ideas came from the school and its students, not from those who happened to teach there.", Email from John Meunier to Patrick Lynch, 25th November, 2019.

16   Cf. ".. my shorthand description of the Caldecote house as Palladian/Brutalist/Usonian. You are absolutely correct in Identifying Wittkower as the agent of that first influence. Other influences are also identified, but the list could be even longer. You barely mention Liverpool, which was certainly the first place where I began to take on board

the larger cultural responsibilities of architecture. Peter Foggo was still there and had mounted an exhibition to parallel the 1955 issue of the Architectural Review called Outrage. No longer there were Jim Stirling and Colin Rowe but they also represented a kind of architectural/cultural seriousness still present in the School. It was from there that I took an Easter vacation to Paris where I visited a lot of Le Corbusier buildings including a still ruined Villa Savoie and the brand new Jaoul Houses where M. Jaoul invited me inside and let me take photographs. It was also while I was a student that I spent a summer after 3rd year interning in London in Hugh Casson's Office (working on Sidgewick Avenue in Cambridge), but perhaps more importantly visited the This Is Tomorrow Exhibition at the Whitechapel Art Gallery where I was very impressed by the Patio and Pavilion exhibit by the Smithsons and Eduardo Paolozzi. You do mention my year-and-a-half long internship between the 4th and the 5th year when was in New York with Marcel Breuer but also hugely important was the 3 month Vespa Scooter tour of the USA when, amongst a lot else, I really discovered Frank Lloyd Wright with visits to the Hollyhock Barnsdall House in LA and the original Taliesin, while also discovering America, my future home, and its landscape. Before arriving in Cambridge to take up an Assistant Lectureship and then build the Caldecote house, there was, of course, the Harvard experience which you do refer to very nicely with Giedeon and Mumford, Chris Alexander, Serge and Peter Chermayeff on Community and Privacy, but there was also Jose Luis Sert and a brief exposure to Le Corbusier while he was working on the Carpenter Center. My class made a visit to New Canaan where we visited a slew of modern houses including Elliot Noyes' house (photo attached), Breuer's own house, and Johnson's Glass House. The latter had a major impact on my thinking about the relationship a house could have to the surrounding landscape which is "reflected" in Caldecote. Between Harvard and Cambridge was the two year experience of living and working in Munich with Fred Angerer, a professor at the Technische Hochschule in Industrie Bau und Kleine Stadtebau. It was there that I learnt a lot about paying attention to how buildings are made, which I think is reflected in the thoughtful detailing of Caldecote. It was also there that I learnt to draw with a mapping pen that responded to the grain of the paper and could be used for drawing the trees and the people as well as the lettering lending a quality to the drawings which is the opposite of mechanical, a method I used for the drawings of the Essex Sports Pavilion and the Burrell Museum. But living in the middle of Europe within driving distance of Paris, Vienna and Venice obviously expanded our cultural references. Lastly is Cambridge itself. Although I began designing Caldecote

almost as soon as we arrived in 1962—I was initially on a 5 year limited contract—there can be no denying its influence and particularly the influence of Leslie Martin and his lieutenant Colin St. John Wilson (Sandy). It was Sandy who introduced me to Christian Norberg Schultz. And then, of course, I have to mention your favorite antagonist, Peter Eisenman, who was finishing his PhD thesis The Formal Basis of Modern Architecture, which he had begun under the influence of his mentor and my predecessor Colin Rowe, who as you mention was a student of Wittkower; which is where we began." Email from John Meunier to Patrick Lynch, 28th October 2019.

17 See the introduction to *Civic Ground: Rhythmic Spatiality and the Communicative Movements between Architecture, Sculpture and Site*, Patrick Lynch, Artifice Books on Architecture, London, 2017.

18 A number of students at The Liverpool School of Architecture joined the Parachute Regiment during World War II, including James Stirling and Colin Rowe. Rowe in fact blamed his decision to swap the drawing board for a desk on an injury sustained during a practise jump. See for example *Big Jim: The Life and Work of James Stirling*, Mark Girouard, Chatto and Windus, London, 1998 and Rowe, Op. Cit.

19 See "Foothold", above and Op. Cit.

20 *As I Was Saying: Recollections and Miscellaneous Essays*, Volume One

Texas, Pre-Texas, Cambridge, Colin Rowe, MIT, p.131. Rowe is actually citing, from memory (he wrote the essay in 1994) a conversation between himself, Peter Eisenman and Clinton Rossiter, a visiting scholar ("I imagine something like political theory") from Cornell ("it must have been in 1961, perhaps in October, that I made a little dinner...", etc.). The phrase "Fenland Tech" is attributed to Rossiter, along with "the colleges of Cambridge were "no more than the Potemkin villages of education". Rowe continues:"the punchline of the whole evening: "To leave Oxford for Cambridge is like leaving an overblown but neglected rose garden for a horticultural research station in the wilds of Siberia." So, if I didn't necessarily agree with his details, I still applauded his state of mind.", Ibid., p. 132.

21 See *The Other Tradition of Modern Architecture: The Uncompleted Project*, Colin St John Wilson, John Wiley and Sons, London, 1995; "Sigurd Lewerentz and the Dilemma of Classicism", Colin St John Wilson, in *Sigurd Lewerentz 1885-1975: The Dilemma of Classicism*, eds. Alison and Peter Smithson, Hakon Ahlberg, Architectural Association, London, 1989; *Architectural Reflections: Studies in the Philosophy and Practice of Architecture*, Colin St John Wilson, Butterworth-Heinemann, London, 1998; and *Colin St John Wilson: Buildings and Projects*, Roger Stonehouse and Eric Parry, Black Dog Publishing, 2007.

22 See for example Peter Carl's letter, "The grid and the block", written in response to certain contributions to a special issue of Architecture Research Quarterly (arq) devoted to the work of Leslie Martin (edited by the then head of department at Cambridge, Peter Carolin, Volume 4, December 2000): "When given the opportunity to reread Leslie Martin's article, "The grid as generator" (arq 4/4), and the letters that it attracted (arq 5/1), I found myself moving in two levels: the archaeology of the Cambridge School of Architecture, and the problems of urban design. As to the first of these, there seems to be general agreement that Martin established architecture on a properly theoretical foundation, and that he did so in a cultured, humane way. This is a recognizable attribute of Cambridge scientists of the period, for whom it was a moral principle to sustain a rigorously theoretical clarity in one's discipline, as part of a richly developed cultural life. (Jeremy) Till is correct to situate the architectural aspects of the proposition within the context of the Oxford Conference; but, in terms of local archaeology, the presence of Colin Rowe should be added to the scene. The grid was a theme of the period and Rowe's effort to adduce a political value to the grid of New York should be compared with Martin's rendering of the same city. Lastly on Cambridge archaeology, (David) Porter's declaration that the legacy of Martin was disrupted by the emphasis of (Joseph) Rykwert and (Dalibor) Vesely on "history" is a bad

misrepresentation. To the extent there was a disruption, it would be better to say that it lay in taking urban culture more seriously than urban theory. In any case, the latter grows out of the former. As to the discussion regarding the urban grid, there seem to be three principal levels to the argument: a) urban order can be rendered by theories of a type well known from science; b) Martin's discussion of the urban grid is exemplary of such a theory (in fact it is two theories, one on the grid, the other on the perimeter block); and c) such theories, and this one in particular, would provide a useful framework for design research as well as practice. That certain aspects of urban order can be clarified by scientific analysis can be accepted; but there inevitably results a problem of reconciling such styles of thought with the full richness of urban culture (the same could be said of aesthetic theories, and the tediously reiterated choice between aesthetics and science distorts the question)... This style of theory is meant to legitimate and to guide practice; and there is no question that much of the culturally-based theory of recent years is less helpful than that of Martin. However, history demonstrates that culture cannot be made into a project of this kind. The most significant aspects of urban order—which might be understood as a structure for the mediation of conflict—intrinsically resist simulation, systematic or otherwise (the best approximation is found in the Ulysses of Joyce). While there will always be a

place for speculation, in which theories are both hypotheses and potential guides for practice, one's architectural or urban intelligence grows from within practical life, like one's language. If a city be regarded a topography of the practical life, a theory oriented about morphology can always only be a very partial and fragmentary illumination of urban order. It appears that Martin's contribution within the school and the discipline conformed to this view; and it is only the followers or revivalists who would elevate such a theory beyond its true status.", arq . vol 5 . no 2, Cambridge University Press, 2001. Carl recently observed that a number of his colleagues at Harvard GSD have enquired about Lionel March, seeing his work as seminal for paramemtric computational design, Email to the author, 26th November 2019.

23 *Architectonics of Humanism: Essays on Number in Architecture*, Lionel March, Academy Editions, London, 1998.

24 *The Architecture of Form,* Lionel March, Cambridge University Press, 1976. "March was the first director of the Centre for Land Use and Built Form Studies, now the Martin Centre for Architectural and Urban Studies, Cambridge University. He held professorships in systems engineering at the University of Waterloo, Ontario; in design technology at the Open University, Milton Keynes; and from 1984 in the Graduate School of Architecture and Urban Planning, UCLA, where he was the chair in the period 1985–1991 and was professor

emeritus in design and computation until his death."

25 This project was published as "Whitehall: a plan for the national and government centre", Leslie Martin and Colin Buchanan, H.M. Stationery Office, London, 1965. See also *Demolishing Whitehall: Leslie Martin, Harold Martin and the Architecture of White Heat* by Adam Sharr and Stephen Thornton, Ashgate, 2013.

26 "The Grid as Generator", Leslie Martin and Lionel March (1972), republished in *arq*, Volume 4, December 2000.

27 See *Genius Loci: Towards a Phenomenology of Architecture*, Christian Norberg Schulz, Rizzoli, New York 1980. This was in fact also published by Rizzoli's sister press, Electa, the year before in Milan, in 1979.

28 See Peter Carl, Op. Cit.

29 See "Foothold", above, and Op. Cit, p.15.

30 See "Foothold", above. Meunier also recently stated: "The decision not to paint the bricks, as was originally intended, was an aesthetic judgement. The artist wife of my partner noticed that the bricks contained the colour palette of the rest of the materials and gave me pause to reconsider the decision. I then decided not too because I agreed with her about the colours, but also because I found that doing so lent the house a much stronger character, and the achievement of a powerful architecture with the most modest of means was the story of the house.", Email to Hans Munthe-Kaas, 22nd November 2019.

31 See for example *An Architecture of Invitation: Colin St John Wilson*, Sarah Menin and Stephen Kite, Lund Humphries, London, 2005.

32 *The Villa: Form and Ideology of Country Houses*, James S. Ackerman, Princeton University Press, 1990.

33 See also *Villa: From Ancient to Modern*, Joseph Rykwert, Harry N. Abrams, New York, 2000; "All imagination has to be re-imagined: the villa and the architectural imagination", Patrick Lynch, *arq*, volume 9, number 2, 2005; "Sanctified Leisure: The Villa is not a Temple or a Barn: The Villa as Archetype and Paradigm", Patrick Lynch, *The Lives of Spaces: The Irish Pavilion at the Venice Architecture Biennale*, Dublin, 2008.

34 Vesely, Op. Cit. pp. 186-188.

35 Graduates of this course include Daniel Libeskind, Mohsen Mostafavi and David Leatherbarrow.

36 See "Towards a Critical Regionalism: Six points for an architecture of resistance", Kenneth Frampton, in *Anti-Aesthetic: Essays on Postmodern Culture*, ed. Hal Foster, Seattle: Bay Press, 1983; and *Critical Regionalism. Architectural Identity in a Globalized World*, Liane Lefaivre and Alexander Tzonis, Prestel, Munich, 2003, etc.

37 See *Studies in Tectonic Culture: The Poetics of Construction in Nineteenth and Twentieth Century Architecture*, Kenneth Frampton, MIT Press, 2001.

38 Vesely, Op. Cit., 2004, p 106.

39 Ibid, pp 103–104

40 Ibid., p. 106. He continues: "We experience the most obvious manifestations of the structuring role of architecture almost constantly in our everyday lives. There is hardly a place or a circumstance that is not organised by spatial intentions (or in the case of natural surroundings, experienced as organised). The encounter with things and their spatial order is an encounter with the otherness of our situation, accessible through the dialectics of revealing and hiding.... However, we need to see these terms (embodiment and articulation) in their dialectical relationship: it is by resistance that architecture supports our intentions and the appropriate meaning of a situation. We are aware of this most intuitively each time we move up a staircase, travel through uncomfortable corridors, enter rooms with certain expectations, or recognise the purpose of a building from its layout and physiognomy." For a longer discussion of this topic see *Civic Ground: Rhythmic Spatiality and the Communicative Movement between Architecture, Sculpture and Site*, Patrick Lynch, Artifice Books on Architecture, London, 2017.

41 Ibid., pp.48-9 (Vesely is citing Maurice Merleau-Ponty's *Phenomenology of Perception*, translated by Colin Smith, Routledge, London, 1962, p 250).

42   See for example *Phenomenological Psychology*, Erwin Straus, Hachette, New York, 1966; and *Phenomenology of Memory*, Erwin Straus, Duquesne University Press, 1970.

43   Cited in Vesely, Op. Cit., p 82.

44   Ibid., p 106.

45   Ibid., pp 83–84: "The order is always a result of dialogue between the representative structure of space and the spontaneity of natural change, manifested in the changing nature of the seasons, growth and decay of the flora, changing weather."

46   Ibid., p 64.

47   Ibid., pp 66–67.

48   Ibid., pp 77–78.

49   Ibid., p 86.

50   Ibid., p 88.

51   Ibid., pp 106–107. Vesely is citing Martin Heidegger's "The Origin of the Work of Art", *Poetry, Language, Thought*, New York: Harper & Row, 1971.

52   Vesely, Op. Cit, p 91.

53   Ibid., pp 71–73.

54   Ibid., p 72.

55   p 91. Vesely continues: "Resonance... casts light on the spontaneous formation of identities and differences, similarities and analogies, and more generally on the metaphorical nature of all communication. At the same time it is closely linked with rhythm, proportion, and harmony. It is well known that the primary meaning of proportion is analogical; and while analogy belongs to the metaphoricity of discourse, proportion more explicitly represents its structure, which can be eventually expressed in numbers. We do not need to be reminded that proportion was, until recently, at the center of thinking about architecture and its order. But it is not always understood or acknowledged that proportional thinking was primarily mediation between the ideas of a potential unity of the world and the uniqueness of a particular situation or phenomenon. In the history of Western culture, this process became a mediation between the celestial and the terrestrial order, between divine and human reality, and finally between the universal and particular in the understanding of the world." (pp 91–92).

56   Cf. "An amusement exercise for me: How to adapt the Corbusier Modulor to brick measures. It is actually very nice. Brick is (WxDxH): 9"x4.5"x3". Since the base unit of the modulor U=183cm = 6' = 72" is exactly 8W, and 8 is a fibonacci number, it all matches perfectly. The modulor is made from U using the golden ratio f = (1+sqrt(2))/2 = 1.61...

E.g. the stretched out man is U + U/fxfxf = 226cm = 7'6". Best approximations of the golden ratio by rational fractions (division of integers) is obtained from the fibonacci sequence where the new term is the sum of the two previous: 1, 1, 2, 3, 5, 8, 13, 21, 34, 55, ... The ratio between two neighbours in the sequence, like 8/5=1.6 is near f (getting better and better higher up).

So if U=8W, the stretched out man should be 8W+2W = 10W (we have U+U/f*f*f ~= 8W+2W = 10W , since 2 is three steps to right of 8). The 'pure' (powers of f) discrete modulor measures should therefore be: 2, 3, 5, 8, 13, 21, .. brick widths. For heights multiply by 3, depths multiply by 2. Some discrete modulor measures, compared to your house: Unit: 8W Stretched out man: 10W = 20H (exactly the height in the bedroom area). U*f ~= 13W = 39H (the height in living room is actually 40H). U*f*f ~= 21W = 15'9" (the living area is 15'=20W). U*f*f*f*f ~= 55W (the plinth of the house is 40' = 53W). Happy Thanksgiving. -Hans"–Email from Hans Munthe-Kaas to John Meunier, 28th November 2019.

57   See for example the writing of Peter Carl, e.g. "Room as Horizon", in issue 4 of *The Journal of Civic Architecture*, Canalside Press, London, 2019, for a further discussion of the ontological and spatial significance of this term. See also, *Body, Community, Language, World*, Jan Patocka, Open Court, Chicago, 1999.

58   See http://longnow.org/

59   See "Foothold", above and Op. Cit.

Biographies

Simon Henley

is an architect. He studied at the University of Liverpool (1986–1992) where he was awarded the Reilly Medal in 1992, and at the University of Oregon, USA (1990–1991). He combines practice with teaching, writing and research, and is the author of *The Architecture of Parking* (Thames & Hudson, 2007), which won the RIBA International Book Award for Construction in 2008, and *Redefining Brutalism* (RIBA Publications, 2017). Simon is a postgraduate unit master at Kingston University, London, where he has also embarked on a PhD by Practice. He is a Fellow of the Royal Society of Arts and Brother of the Art Workers Guild. Simon is a principal of London-based architecture practice Henley Halebrown. Completed works include Talkback, St. Benedict's School, Hackney New School, the Akerman Health Centre, De Beauvoir Block, Junction Arts & Civic Centre, Copper Lane—London's first co-housing scheme—and the Chadwick Hall student residences. Chadwick Hall was shortlisted for the 2018 RIBA Stirling Prize. 2018 saw the publication of a monograph reflecting on Henley Halebrown's work by Swiss publishers Quart Verlag in their De Aedibus International series.

Patrick Lynch

is an architect based in London. He studied at the universities of Liverpool and Cambridge, completing his PhD at The Cass with Peter Carl, Joseph Rykwert and Helen Mallinson in 2015. He has taught at The Architectural Association, the University of Cambridge, The Cass, and since 2016 has been a Honorary Professor at Liverpool University. He established Lynch Architects in 1997. Recipient of numerous awards, their projects have been widely published and exhibited at major events, including The Venice Biennale in 2012, the Irish pavilion at Venice in 2008, and the Milano Triennale in 2017. Patrick is the author of *Civic Ground* (2017), *Mimesis* (2015), and *The Theatricality of the Baroque City* (2011).

John Meunier

is an architect who studied at the University of Liverpool's School of Architecture in 1953, from which he graduated with a First Class Honours Degree in 1959 having done over a year of practical training in New York with Marcel Breuer in 1957-8. He went on to pursue a Master's degree at Harvard University. He, and his wife then went to Munich where he worked for two years for a Professor at the Technische Universitat. He was then appointed to an Assistant Lectureship the University of Cambridge, where he taught for 14 years. During that time he was also a practicing architect responsible, together with Barry Gasson, for several published buildings including the Burrell Collection in Glasgow. In 1976 he was appointed Director of the School of Architecture and Interior Design at the University of Cincinnati. In 1987 he became Dean of the College of Architecture and Environmental Design at Arizona State University, a position he held for fifteen years. He has been Emeritus Professor of Architecture there since he retired from his professorship in 2017. His interests, reflected in print and on television, have been the architecture and urbanism of desert cities, and Intricacy as an essential characteristic of architecture and the arts.

WITH THANKS TO

This book is the result of a friendship that has grown out of a coming together, on-line, of a handful of architects who were very concerned about what was being planned for the Burrell Collection by Glasgow City Council in 2016. These people include Alan Dunlop (who was very much on the ground in Glasgow and an architectural leader in that community), Deane Hawkes, Richard Waite of the Architects Journal, Robin Ward (who took some very fine photographs of the Burrell), Brit Andresen, etc.

John would like to acknowledge his collaborators: Barry Gasson (the co-author of several projects in this volume); Brit Andresen (co-author of the Burrell), David Handlin (co-author of New Hall), Tom Bader, a senior student at Cincinnati who went on to do a Masters at Yale (collaborator on the Gordon House). And his clients: Dorothy Meunier (The Meunier House), John Wendon (The Wendon House, Barton), Jeff and Jackie Edington (The Edington House), and Lynne Gordon (The Gordon House, Cincinnati).

Patrick would like to acknowledge the invaluable insights, editorial acuity and rigorous advice of David Evans; the wisdom and patience of Emma Kalkhoven; David Grandorge for taking such wonderful photographs of The Meunier House; Simon Henley for his excellent essay and for over 30 years of friendship; Tom Lee for his marvellous photographs of the Burrell, and also for over 30 years of friendship (I met Simon and Tom at Liverpool School of Architecture in 1987); and the loving support and critical tenacity of Claudia Lynch.

Canalside Press
66 Regent Studios
8 Andrews Rd
London E8 4QN
+44 (0)20 7278 2553
info@canalsidepress.com
www.canalsidepress.com

All opinions expressed within this publication
are those of the authors and not necessarily of
the publisher.

Designed by Emma Kalkhoven
Printed by KOPA, Lithuania

British Library Cataloguing-in-Publication Data.
A CIP record for this book is available from the
British Library.

ISBN 978-1-5272-4050-6

Every effort has been made to trace the copyright
holders, but if any have been inadvertently
overlooked the necessary arrangements will be
made at the first opportunity.

PHOTOGRAPHIC CREDITS

Roger Clarke: 16 (top)

John Donat: 259 (bottom)

David Grandorge: cover, 20, 21, 46, 78, 79, 80, 81, 125,
206 (bottom), 209 (bottom), 208, 210, 212, 213, 214–215,
216–217, 218, 219, 220–221, 222, 223, 254–255, 284–285.

Simon Henley: 76, 86, 87, 88, 91, 92, 261 (top).

Tom Lee: 100, 101, 102–103, 106, 107, 108, 109, 110–111, 139.

Patrick Lynch: 12, 32, 33, 34, 200, 208, 224, 225, 232, 247, 249.

Mjollnir MacAlba: 104–105

John Meunier: 16 (bottom), 27, 28,29, 41 42,43, 44, 45, 52
(top), 55, 112, 116, 117, 120, 126 (bottom), 137, 138, 140, 143,
146, 147, 150, 152, 155, 156, 157,158, 166, 170, 171, 172, 173,
174, 177, 180, 185, 186, 190, 199, 206, 209, 239, 240, 252,
260, 261 (middle and bottom), 286

Hans Munthe-Kaas: 226, 252 (top), 282.

Scala Archives: 85

Henk Snoek: 18, 26 (left), 129, 130, 259 (top and middle)

Ray Williams for the Sunday Observer Magazine: 160,
202, 203

Licensed under CC BY 2.0:
Keith Edkins: 135; Jchancerel: 68; Henk de Klerk: 67;
Hay Kranen: 64; Marcok: 52; 99; Bart Molendijk: 73;
Anthony O'Neil: 35, 36, Pschemp: 55; Sailko: 70;
A.J. van der Wahl: 72

Dedication page:
John Meunier and Dorothy Donnelly at Breuer's
Christmas party December 1957. Photographer
unknown.